The Mysterious Marvelous Snowflake

The Mysterious Marvelous Snowflake

and Other Object Lessons for Children

Harvey D. & Patsie S. Moore

Abingdon/Nashville

The Mysterious Marvelous Snowflake
Copyright © 1981 by Abingdon

Library of Congress Cataloging in Publication Data

MOORE, HARVEY DANIEL, 1942–
The mysterious marvelous snowflake.
1. Children's sermons. I. Moore, Patsie S., joint author.
II. Title
BV4315.M625   252'.53   80-20996

ISBN 0-687-27640-3

Scripture quotations are from the Revised Standard
Version of the Bible, copyrighted 1946, 1952, © 1971,
1973 by the Division of Christian Education of the
National Council of the Churches of Christ in the U.S.A.

MANUFACTURED BY THE PARTHENON PRESS AT
NASHVILLE, TENNESSEE, UNITED STATES OF AMERICA

To
Jackie & Shirley,
Marla & Steve
Mote

CONTENTS

INTRODUCTION

There are a number of ways to express the value of children. Jesus said, "To such belongs the kingdom of God," and unless we become as one of them, we will never enter that kingdom. I once heard a psychiatrist explain to a group that if adults work long enough and hard enough, they someday may regain the understanding, empathy, and clarity of perception of the average five-year-old.

We are asked frequently what we think the children's moment in worship gives to the children. We feel it gives a great deal. Of equal importance, though asked less frequently, What do the service and the adults gain from the children? It is our belief that the children add a tremendous amount to the worship experience—not as entertainment, or because they are cute, but because their questions and insights tend to cut through the tenuously hung facades of the adult world and bring us back to the basic issues of interpersonal relationships and honest personal examination.

In light of that observation, the first thing we would suggest in talking with the children is that you take them seriously. Children are extremely perceptive and very anxious to please. If they sense that you are there to entertain the adults, they will give you what you want. If your attitude and mannerisms convey a stiff sort of formality and a desire to "get it over with," they will sense that also.

On the other hand, if you convey to them an honest personal interest by actually listening to their responses, they will share with you and the congregation the gift of purity of spirit and openness of love that caused Jesus to hold them up as examples.

Each talk that follows is designed to explore one specific question or one aspect of the child's life. We have done that for a reason. One of the great problems in teaching, or in discussions, is that we tend to include a wide variety of material or ideas, but we never really develop and mine that one central concept. The teaching object of these talks, then, is twofold. The first is for the children to gain a real insight through personal give-and-take—to be able to say, "I figured that out. Now it makes sense." The second purpose is to bring about some means of specific application of the concept that is being presented. A lesson has not been learned thoroughly until it has been experienced.

The ultimate goal of each contact with the children is to share the message of God's love for them. We consider it one of the world's great tragedies that children, in whom there is so much love, are entrusted to systems and to individuals who attempt to manipulate them through fear and threats, sometimes thinly disguised as religion.

The moments we spend with the children should be times to hear and to be involved with their concerns and their struggles and to join with each of them in that awesome journey of growth and in the joy of discovery. Those moments can form a bond that is unlike any other. It is a time of sharing and acceptance, and if we are honest with ourselves, it can be a time of *mutual* growth.

Above all else, the integrity and value of each child as an individual should be strengthened. Each is of ultimate value, and the thrust of the talk and the manner of presentation always should reaffirm their individuality as well as their common heritage of God's love.

In a world where there are endless sources of negative comment and poor advice that will chain a child to a mediocre existence, it is our role and great joy to provide the keys to the locks and the wings to fly free.

Sitting in a Cage . . .

TEXT: But someone will say, "You have faith and I have works." Show me your faith apart from your works, and I by my works will show you my faith. *James 2:18*

OBJECT: A cat in a large birdcage.

THRUST: A person doesn't become a Christian just by sitting in a church.

(When you bring the cage out, have it covered with a pillowcase, or some other material, so that the children cannot see the cat.)

I have something very special with me this morning. As some of you know, I enjoy birds, and we feed lots of them in our backyard. This morning I want to share one of my favorites with you. It is frightened easily and that is why I put the cover over the cage. Let's be very quiet and I will lift the cover.

(As you slowly lift the cover, you can continue to describe the unique nature of this "bird." You will begin to get a response from the children as soon as they get their first glimpse. Let them enjoy the discovery for a few seconds.

What's the problem? Don't you like my bird? *(Let them explain the obvious fact that it is not a bird.)*

Kristin says it isn't a bird. Can you believe that? Of course it's a bird! I can prove it. *(That should draw a challenge.)* All right, let me ask you. What is this? *(Point to the cage.)* Right! It's a birdcage. Now what goes in a birdcage? Right! Birds!

Now, my friend here is in a birdcage, so it must be a bird. *(Let the children respond. Some of them may want to present their own arguments as to why your logic does not hold up. That's fine.)*

Let me see if I understand what you are saying. Just sitting in a birdcage doesn't make something a bird. Is that it? Right. What makes a bird a bird is the way it lives, the way it looks, acts, and a lot of other things. At least those are the things I've heard you say. Well, I must admit, I agree with you.

I would like you to carry your discovery one step farther, however. Sitting in a birdcage doesn't make a cat a bird, and sitting in a church doesn't make a person a Christian! Did you ever think about that?

There are a lot of people who feel that if they come to church once a week, they are Christians. But they are like our cat in the birdcage. What makes us Christians is not where we sit, but what we believe, and the way those beliefs are acted out in our lives. It's what we do that tells people what we really are and what we believe.

So this week, let's give some thought to the way we act. Are we *being* Christians? Are we *doing* the things that are part of being a Christian, or are we like the cat—claiming the name, but being something quite different?

Do You Think
God Knows When We Aren't
Telling the Truth?

TEXT: If we say we have no sin, we deceive ourselves,
          and the truth is not in us. If we confess our sins,
          he is faithful and just, and will forgive our sins
          and cleanse us from all unrighteousness.
          I John 1:8-9

OBJECT: A loaf of bread.

THRUST: When we are attempting to deceive someone, we
          usually are far more obvious than we imagine. It
          is better simply to admit our errors and accept
          forgiveness.

I have a loaf of bread with me because it is the center of a
wild experience I had, and I would like to tell you about it. I
was at the office the other day, and Patsie called. She wanted
me to bring home a loaf of bread from the store. Now, that's no
big problem. I am sure many of you have been asked to get
things for your parents or friends. *(If you can keep the children
identifying with the various aspects of the story line it will
carry more impact.)*

After I hung up the phone, things really got busy, and to be
perfectly honest, I just plain forgot the bread. Have any of you
ever done that? *(There should be an abundance of heads
nodding.)* Well, you probably know how I felt. You may even
suspect what I did. I went into the house and said, "You will
never guess what happened. I was just about to go into the
store to get the bread when a huge dinosaur thundered into

15

the parking lot and almost smashed the car. It was all I could do to escape with my life!" You know what? She didn't believe me. *(Let the children respond with their comments.)* Well, you seem to have some of the same doubts she did. So I'll tell you the truth. This is what actually happened: I bought the bread, and as I was walking home, a five-thousand-pound gorilla swung down out of a tree and grabbed it out of my hand. I almost got it back, but he ate it at the last second. What do you think of that? *(The children should be in the spirit of the story by now and have their comments ready.)*

Well, she didn't believe that one, either, any more than you do. I thought it was a pretty good story. Then I said I would tell her the real truth. I said—"I forgot about it." You know what happened then? She believed me. I wonder why she believed that, and not the other things? *(Let the children give a full response. It will provide the basis for the final point.)*

I think you are right. When I was making up stories it was pretty obvious, even though at the time I thought they were very good. When I told the truth and said I was sorry, she accepted my mistake, and that was the end of it.

I'll tell you what I am wondering. I wonder if it is as obvious to God when we are making up excuses. We know God is a great deal smarter than we are, and he knows a lot about us. Do you think that maybe our excuses don't fool him any more than they fool other people? *(Let them respond so you can see if they have made the shift. There may be some resistance.)*

I don't know about you, but sometimes I find myself doing something I know I shouldn't be doing, and then my temptation is to make up some excuse for it and try to explain it to God that way.

Now, since the story about the bread, I wonder if it might not be better just to say, "God, I made a mistake. I know I shouldn't have done it, and with your help I won't do it again."

Do you think that might be a better way to deal with those situations?

I think you are right. Let's just admit our mistakes and say thanks to God for loving us even when we mess up. We can get rid of the bad feelings and be happy we still are loved.

I Just Don't Understand

TEXT: When a man's folly brings his way to ruin, his heart rages against the Lord. *Proverbs 19:3*

OBJECT: A baseball.

THRUST: Some acts have a natural and predictable consequence. It is not that God is "picking on" us when we experience the results of something we ourselves have set in motion.

I want to tell you about something that happened last week with this baseball. Patti and Nikki and I had gathered up several children on the block, and we were playing baseball. We were having a great time, when all of a sudden God came on the scene and spoiled everything. In fact, he ruined my whole day. *(You may pause for a moment here just to get the reaction. The comment will probably take the children off guard.)*

Craig, you look a little uncertain about that. Let me tell you how it happened; then it will be very clear.

The game was going well, and it was my turn at bat. I got a really good hit, and the ball went all the way across the lot and straight for the neighbor's window. Do you know what happened then? *(The children should be able to identify totally with this situation.)* Right! God broke Mrs. Jones' window. Pushed the ball right through it. That was when God ruined my whole day! What do you think of that? *(At this point the discussion can be very insightful. The children are*

18

well aware of the identity of the person who broke the window, but they probably have been exposed to the line of reasoning that conveniently shifts all responsibility for our actions onto God or the devil or somebody else.)

As I listen to this discussion I get the feeling that Gene doesn't think God did it. In fact, I heard Daniel say that *I* did it. I thought if God wanted that window to be in one piece he would have kept it that way. If he chose not to protect it, he must have wanted it broken. Right? *(Let the children wrestle with the problem a little longer.)*

The message I hear coming through is that if I hit a ball straight at a window, it's my action, and I shouldn't blame it on God. Is that right? I thought so.

I wonder . . . have you ever been around folks who ask questions such as, "Why did God let that dog get hit by the car?" or "Why does God let children starve in some places?" Have you heard questions like that? *(Let the children join freely at this point. You may discover that they are wondering about some rather profound things but have been uncertain about how to phrase them.)*

Some of you seem to think that before we blame God for the dog being hit, we ought to ask why he was in the street, and if the driver really was paying attention. I think you are right. In fact, in light of our discussion, I suspect that we really may be responsible for a lot of the things we blame on God.

This week, I would like you to listen to what you say and pray. When you ask God why things happen or why they don't happen, stop and ask what you could do to help. Maybe God wants things different, and that's why he put you where you can change them.

But I Had Good Intentions . . .

TEXT: Do not withold good from those to whom it is due, when it is in your power to do it.   *Proverbs 3:27*

OBJECT: A Christmas card, a birthday card, or whatever fits the occasion.

THRUST: It is never too late to do something nice or kind.

(The card used in this particular talk was a Christmas card, postmarked December 26.)

I would like to share something with you this morning that I think is really great. I suspect all of you know what this is. *(Hold up the card.)* Right! It's a Christmas card. Now, I enjoy getting cards, but this one gave me a sort of special joy. I would like some of you to take a moment and look carefully at the envelope. Do you notice anything different about it? *(The children may come up with several thoughts. Give them some time to look carefully.)*

Kristin got it! If you look carefully, you will notice that this Christmas card was mailed on December 26! That's the day *after* Christmas. *(If you use a real situation, I suggest you check it out with the sender first to avoid embarrassment.)*

Now, I thought that was really interesting, and I'll tell you why. The person who sent this card might have looked at the calendar and said, "I'm just too late. Christmas is past, so I won't send it now." Have any of you ever done that? Have you started to do something for someone and then decided it was too late and so you didn't do it? *(Some of the children may have had this happen to them or are aware of times when it happened to others. Let them share their experiences.)*

I think a lot of us fall into that trap. We do something we shouldn't and we don't apologize; then we begin thinking it's too late, and we never do it. Maybe we plan to help someone, and we don't do it at the time we planned, so we just forget it. The result is, we never get it done, and the other person never has the joy of knowing what we were thinking or of receiving what we wanted to share.

If the sender of this card had said, "Oh, it's too late, I'll just wait until next year," I would not have had this card to enjoy.

This is what I think we all can learn from this card and from the person who sent it: It is never too late to do something thoughtful or kind. So if you ever find yourself saying, "Oh, I meant to do that, but now it's too late," stop and think for a moment. If it is a kind thing to do, go ahead and do it. It's never to late to do something nice!

What Do You Want Me to Be????

TEXT: A friend loves at all times. *Proverbs 17:17*

OBJECT: The children.

THRUST: It is a self-defeating process to attempt to live our lives according to the expectations of others.

(One of the great difficulties that children have—and retain as adults—is attempting to live in a manner that will "please" others. They often are given overt or subtle messages that say, "I will like you if you do what I tell you." It leaves the child in a difficult position—trying to determine how to act in order to win love or friendship that, if it were really valid, should be given freely. To prepare for this talk you need to give simple instructions ahead of time to four of your children. Their lines will be "Stand up," "Sit down," "Sit by the piano," and "Stand by the speaker," respectively.)

This morning I would like a helper. Oh, great! You really are an eager group. We should have a good time with this much energy. Dustin, you had your hand up very quickly; will you be the helper? Good. Now, the rest of you may want to help out, because Dustin is going to need some *good* advice. Dustin, what I want you to do is very simple. Just follow the instructions you are given. I want you to keep everyone happy. That's all there is to it.

Nikki, what would you like Dustin to do? "Stand up." Well, that's easy enough. All you have to do to make Nikki happy is stand up. Now remember, you have to keep her happy. You're doing fine.

Renea, what would you like Dustin to do? "Sit by the piano." That's a good one. *(As the child begins to obey, you may have to clarify his problem for him.)* Dustin, you may have to think about that for a minute. You can go to the piano, but if you sit, you will make Nikki unhappy. She wants you to stand. What are you going to do? *(Let him offer some suggestions and get advice from the other children. Include as many as possible.)*

Well, there seems to be a compromise being offered. If you *stand* by the piano, you will be doing part of what each of them wants. That will leave Renea a little unhappy though. She wants you to sit.

Mark, what would make you happy? Now that's a real problem. To make Mark happy you have to come and stand by me. If you do that, Nikki may feel OK, but Renea is really going to be unhappy. You won't be by the piano, or sitting. What are you going to do about that?

(Let all the children get into the advice. They may come up with some ingenious solutions.)

I can see you really have a problem, and you are already at a point where you can't keep everyone happy. Now would you believe that Kristin wants you to sit down? If you do that you will have Nikki unhappy. Now what? *(By this time the problem ought to be obvious, as well as the impossibility of solving it. Dustin is in a hopeless position.)*

Dustin, come sit down for a minute, and let's all take a look at what happened. Dustin started out by trying to do all the things that would make other people like him. Do you ever find yourselves doing that? Sure, we do it all the time, don't we? But look what happened. He kept having more and more things said to him, and he couldn't do them all. Different people wanted him to be and do different things. Do you ever find that happening to you when you are busy "pleasing" people? (*Let the children relate from their own experience and frustration.*)

Right! It really is impossible, isn't it? What do you think Dustin could do? Sure, John has a good idea. Dustin could do what *he* wants to do. If people really like us for who we are, they won't put conditions on their friendship—such as, "I'll like you if you give me a pencil," or "I'll be your friend if you will eat lunch with me."

That doesn't mean we should ignore the things that make others happy, but it does mean that we should learn to be who we are. God made each of us special, with our own talents and abilities, and to develop them, we have to be free to be ourselves.

This week, when you catch yourself trying to be something you really aren't just to please someone else, remember that you are *you*, and if people really like you, they will like you as you are. It is important to be the *best* you you can be, but be *you*.

Also, remember that everyone else has that right, too. So if you find yourself telling someone else, "I'll like you if . . . ," stop and think about what you are saying.

This week, remember God made you to be you, so be the best you that you can be.

Getting a Good Start

TEXT: When you reap the harvest of your land, you shall
         not reap your field to its very border, neither shall
         you gather the gleanings after your harvest. And
         you shall not strip your vineyard bare, neither
         shall you gather the fallen grapes . . . you shall
         leave them for the poor. *Leviticus 19:9-10*

OBJECT: A Monopoly game and a picture of hungry
         children.

THRUST: Some children do not have the advantages that
         others may have when they start out in life.

I know that some of you have seen this game before. Can anyone tell me what it is? Right. It is a Monopoly game. How many of you have seen one, or know how to play? Good. We have a few here who have played before, so you will be able to help me as we go.

Really, it is a simple game. The idea is that we all start out with some play money, and as we move around the board, we buy different squares. Then if other people land on our squares, they have to pay us. The more squares we own, the more money we get, and if we own enough squares, we will get all the money and win the game. As you can see, it is important to be able to buy some of the squares at the beginning, before they are all gone. Does everyone get the basic idea? Good. Now, since we have to have money to buy the squares, I will begin by passing it out. *(Begin counting out the money and keep talking. You can make the point without ever actually distributing the money. Direct your comments to the older children first, because they will catch the problem most quickly.)*

While I am counting, I will explain the process. David will get $5,000. That sure sounds like a lot. Marla, you can have $500. You can buy something with that. Let's see. Eva, you can have $3 and Audra can have $10,000. *(By this time all the children should be well aware that something is wrong with the system, and comments should be flowing freely.)*

I get the distinct feeling that some of you are not happy with the way we are dividing up the money. Why is that? *(Let them give full expression to the problem.)*

As I listen to all this, I must admit that you seem to have a good point. It really doesn't seem very fair, does it? In fact, that is exactly what I would like to talk about this morning. We are all starting out in a sort of big game—only it really isn't a game. It is called life. Most of us are starting out in pretty good shape. We have been given a number of things that most people never even dream of having. If you look at this picture you can see that these children are starting the game with no food. We are given an abundance, but they have very little. Some children have no schools. They have no chance to learn so that they can get a good job. Others have no one to care for them, or they have no home. They are starting the game, but they are already way behind. How would you feel if you were in their place? *(Let the children express their feelings and recommendations.)*

Most of you seem to feel it isn't very fair. How do you think you could change that? Shawna says that those who have a lot can share with the ones who don't have so much. How do you feel about that idea? *(Let the discussion flow for a time.)* It does sound like the kind of thing Jesus would like us to do.

How can we share with those children? (*It may take a few seconds, but the ideas will come. You may want to have some specific suggestions ready, also.*) I have heard some good ideas. We can share part of our allowance so they can buy food. We can save stamps and send them to the outreach program for milk. We can have our class adopt a child. There are all sorts of ways. You really came up with some great ideas!

This week, whenever you thank God for all the good things you have, stop for just a moment and ask God what you can do to share with those who are less fortunate. Then do it! Let's help everyone get a fair start in God's beautiful world.

This Apple Tastes Bad!

TEXT: Just then his disciples came. They marveled that he was talking with a woman, but none said, "What do you wish?" or, "Why are you talking with her?" *John 4:27*

OBJECT: An apple that is rotten inside.

THRUST: It is a dangerous practice to judge a large group of people or objects by your experience of only a few.

I would like to know if some of you would be willing to help me this afternoon with a special project. I want to get everyone together, and we are going to drive through the area and cut down all the apple trees we can find. Then we are going to go to all the stores and have them throw away all the apples they have. I think that is really a worthwhile project. Jeff, you look a little puzzled. I guess I ought to give you a reason, and I have a good one.

Today I wanted to enjoy a quick snack, and I decided on an apple. You know what I discovered? Apples are rotten. Look at this. (*Hold up the apple and let them see the brown spot inside.*) There you have it. That's my reason, and it is based on firsthand experience. Apples are rotten, and we ought to get rid of them before someone else has the same thing happen to them that happened to me.

Patti, you look as if you don't agree. What is the problem? (*Several children may want to comment at this point, so let them share their thoughts.*) Nikki, are you telling me that I shouldn't judge all apples by just one? Do the rest of you feel that way? *(Let them reaffirm their position.)* Well, I must admit you make a pretty good case. It really would be silly to say that just because one apple isn't good, all apples are bad. We never would do that seriously, would we?

But I am wondering why we do it with people, if we know better than to do it with apples? Have you ever thought about how many times Jesus had to deal with that exact problem? People met tax collectors they didn't like, so they said that *all* tax collectors were bad. Yet Matthew was a tax collector, and Jesus loved him. People met some Romans they didn't like, and they said they were all bad; yet Jesus talked about the great faith of a Roman soldier and said that others should be like him. Time and time again, people made that mistake, and Jesus always was having to tell them not to judge others by some preconceived ideas.

Today we even hear some people say they don't come to church because they know a church member who acts in a way he shouldn't. They judge all Christians by one or two. That not only is unfair, it's silly.

Jesus said that all of us are God's children and that we must be seen as individuals. This week, when you find yourself beginning to make one of those statements, remember the apple, and ask, "Do I really know *this* person as an individual and as a child of God, or am I judging by what I 'think' might be the case?" Then let's get to know a person as God's Special Child before we decide what he or she is like.

I Like Trash!

TEXT: And forgive us our debts, as we also have forgiven our debtors. . . . For if you forgive men their trespasses, your heavenly Father also will forgive you; but if you do not forgive men their trespasses, neither will your Father forgive your trespasses.   *Matthew 6:12, 14-15*

OBJECT: A plastic garbage bag filled with a variety of trash.

THRUST: We sometimes tend to hang onto emotional "trash"—that is, bad feelings—that would be better thrown away.

I really am glad you are all here today, because I have some great things to show you. I have an entire sack full of *trash!* *(Open the sack and let them see the contents.)* Isn't that great? There are old soup cans, lots of torn-up paper, and even some potato peels and leftover oatmeal. *It is fantastic!* I like it so much I am going to go home and lay it all out on the floor of my room. Wouldn't that be something? Can you imagine getting up at night and stepping into a big blob of cold oatmeal? *(That should draw a number of comments, all unfavorable.)*

Nikki, you don't seem to think that is such a great idea. Why not? *(There may be several children who have specific comments.)* Well it's obvious that most of you don't think you would like this in your room. I guess it would be kind of silly to take a nice pretty room and fill it with garbage and trash. It surely would smell bad.

Have you ever thought about the kind of trash we do keep? I mean trash like bad feelings. For example, I met someone yesterday who really felt bad. Here it was a beautiful day, with lots of things to do, and she felt "blah." I asked what the problem was, and she said that a few days before, a friend had called her a name. Now, I know that she might feel bad about that, but after two days, it ought to be forgiven, forgotten, and set aside. Carrying around a "feel bad" is like filling our room with trash. It really messes up the place, and after a while it even keeps us from doing good things when we have a chance. Have any of you ever found yourselves walking around remembering things that have happened and then feeling bad about them all over again? *(You may get some good insights into the children at this point. It also may open some areas for you to follow up individually.)*

It sounds as if several of you have done that, and it doesn't leave you feeling very good. What I would suggest is when something happens and you feel bad about it, go ahead and deal with it right then. Get the feelings taken care of; then move on. If you made a mistake, admit it. Remember, God loves you and will help you start over. If someone has hurt your feelings, remember how many times God has forgiven you, and then forget it and move on. Whenever you find yourself starting to dig back through the "feel bad" trash, stop and say, "What am I doing, playing in this trash can?" Then throw it away and think of all the great things you can do. Let's throw out the trash and enjoy the good life God gives us.

Watch Me Get Ready

TEXT: For he says, "At the acceptable time I have listened to you, and helped you on the day of salvation." Behold, now is the acceptable time; behold, now is the day of salvation.
II Corinthians 6:2

OBJECT: A stop watch, or a watch with a sweep second hand.

THRUST: Sometimes we spend so much time in preparation, we never get the job done.

This morning I have something really great to show you. It won't take long, but I think you will like it. Will one of you help me by keeping up with the time? (*Be sure to select one of the older children who can read the second hand.*)

Nikki is going to keep an eye on the watch for me. I only have one minute to do this, but that is plenty of time. Nikki, are you ready? Good. Tell me when the minute is up. We can start now. (*Most children in this age group have some anxiety about being "timed," so when the child with the watch starts calling out the time, they begin to get uneasy if you don't hurry.*)

Now I only have fifty seconds left, so I need to get ready to do this. First I need to roll up my sleeves. (*Slowly push up your sleeves and do several other things that appear to be "preparation." The children will become increasingly uneasy as the time grows shorter.*)

Now, I think I'm just about ready. Nikki, did you say something? Time is up? That can't be . . . I haven't done anything yet. *(At this point you can have some fun with the child keeping the watch.)* Can that be right? I spent all my time getting ready, and I never got to do what I'd planned! What do you think about that? *(You should receive a number of comments from the children.)* I agree. It really does seem silly to spend so much time getting ready that we never get around to doing the thing we're getting ready for. But that is a rather common problem. In fact, if you think about it for a moment, you may even be able to remember a time when you did it. Sometimes, I think we may fall into that trap when we work in the church. We see lots of things that need to be done—people need to be fed, the sick visited, new people welcomed—all sorts of things. We see them, and we know we ought to do something, but we hesitate. First we plan, then we think, then we talk it over, and you know what has happened by the time we have done all this? Right. The time has passed and it is too late.

This week, when you see an opportunity to help or to share with someone, *do it! Now* is the time! Go ahead, and see what great things happen!

The Mysterious Marvelous Snowflake

TEXT: And his gifts were that some should be apostles, some prophets, some evangelists, some pastors and teachers, to equip the saints for the work of ministry, for building up the body of Christ, until we all attain to the unity of the faith and of the knowledge of the Son of God, to mature manhood, to the measure of the stature of the fulness of Christ. *Ephesians 4:11-17*

OBJECT: A lightweight square of white paper, and scissors. First fold your paper in half. Then fold it in half again; then fold it one more time, into a triangle. Now snip out several bits from each side of the triangle. Be sure to leave some space between each snip. You now have a paper snowflake. This procedure should be done while you are talking to the children. A picture of a field covered with snow is also helpful. *Snow Crystals*, by Wilson Bentley, is a good source of pictures.

THRUST: God made us, like the snowflakes, each different, each unique, and each with its own beauty.

Winter is one of my favorite times of year. I enjoy the snow and all the things that go with it, and I especially enjoy looking at the beauty of the snowfields, as far as you can see. Have any of you ever looked out over the fields after a snow, or have you seen a picture of wide fields covered with a fresh snowfall?

You may have seen one that looked like this. *(Hold up the picture. There are many children who never have seen what you are describing, so the picture is important.)*

Have any of you ever seen or played in a field like this? *(Let them relate their own experiences and get into the flow of the talk.)*

What I want to talk about this morning is not so much the snowmen or the snowballs, but the snow itself. *(Begin making your snowflake as you talk.)*

Have any of you ever seen just one lone snowflake? They really are fascinating. In fact, the snowflake is a mystery for a number of reasons. First, the flake is always a flat, six-sided shape. It always has a hexagonal pattern with either six sides or six points. And the most interesting thing of all about the snowflake is that no two ever have been found to be exactly alike. Did you know that snowflakes measuring more than an inch in diameter are not uncommon? And did you know that the biggest snowflake in the world supposedly fell in Montana in 1887 and was fifteen inches in diameter and eight inches thick?! Some snowflake!

A man named Wilson Bentley of Jericho, Vermont, devoted his whole life to the work of photographing snowflakes. He made six thousand photographs . . . and he *never* found two alike! Nor has anyone else. Why do you think God makes them all different?

(This is a fun question, and can draw some great answers. It also helps to get some of the children thinking along the lines of "why" God does a tremendous number of things that we never ponder or truly appreciate, because we take them for granted.)

Well, we have had some fun looking at the differences in snowflakes, but there are other things that are different too. Just as there are no two snowflakes alike, neither are there any two people who are alike. Every person in the whole world is one of a kind. We have lots of things in common, just like the snow. But also like the flakes, each of us is completely unique.

That is a really interesting thing to think about when you meet a new person. Here is someone who is different from everyone else in the whole world! What can that person teach us? And what can we teach and share? It's a great experience. But there's one more thing to remember. If no two people are the same, that means that each of you is one of a kind, as well. No one in all the world is just like you. That makes you someone very special. God has given you a particular set of talents and abilities, and only you can put them together in your own special way.

This week, spend some time looking at the special things that different people can do. Notice how each person has special talents and abilities. Then take some time to discover what your abilities are and what you can do with them. Since God gave you your talents, he might be a good one to ask for advice. You are God's special one-of-a-kind creation. Feel good about it, and with God's help be all you can be.

Let's Play Kickarocco

TEXT: The Ten Commandments. *Exodus 20:1-17*

OBJECT: A kickball.

THRUST: The game is a lot more fun if we all know the rules and follow them.

I have something this morning that I know most of you have seen and used in a number of games. We used to call it a kickball. How many of you have played with one of these? *(Probably all the children will have used one in some context, and they may want to tell you about it.)*

That's great. Roxie said she was on a kickball team. I'll bet that was fun. Brad was on a soccer team. Lots of you have played games with a ball like this. That's good, because that is what I would like to do this morning.

I want to have us play a game of Kickarocco. *(You should get a blank response, because there is no such game.)* Kristin says she would like to play but doesn't know how. Well, that is the really fun part of this game. There are no rules. The players do just as they want. You can score anytime you want, because there are no rules to say how to do it. You can just kick the ball and say you scored a point. Then the other team can kick the ball and say they scored ten points. It's all fair, because there is no rule to say you can't do it. In the last game, I scored five hundred points and Patti only had three. I thought I had won, but she said we were playing that the lowest score won. I wasn't very happy about that, but there are no rules to go by, so who can tell! Anyway, that is a little bit about the way the game works. Does it sound like fun? *(Some of the children may agree just so they can kick the ball. Look to some of your more thoughtful children and you will notice some slight confusion or concern.)*

Ricky, what is the matter? You don't look too sure about all this. What is the problem? *(Let some of them explain the problem as they see it. To make the point with your more competitive children, simply announce that every time they touch the ball it is a point for the other team. If they protest, that's fine. There are no rules to say otherwise.)*

We seem to have a great deal of discussion about this. Derrick, what is the trouble? *(Let one of your more articulate children summarize.)* What I hear you saying is that if we eliminate all the rules, we don't have a game—we just have a mess with a lot of arguments. *(Let the children confirm the statement.)* Well, I think you are right. It sure makes games easier where there are some guidelines we all can go by.

What I would like you to consider is that life is a lot like a game. Have you ever heard someone complain about some of the rules God has set up? *(Several of the children may provide examples.)* Right! We say God keeps telling us *not* to do things, and that's no fun. But actually, God is saying that if we play by his rules, the game will be much better, and there won't be nearly as much fighting and hard feelings.

For instance, God says, "Don't hurt other people." Now, that's a good rule. If we hurt others they probably will hurt us. God says, "Don't steal from other people." That's a good idea because if we do, no one will trust us, and we will have no friends.

In fact, I think if you will look carefully at the rules God gives, you will find that they really are there for our protection, and if you obey them, you will have a lot better time in the game of life.

You're Not Wanted!

TEXT: But Jesus said, "Let the children come to me, and do not hinder them; for to such belongs the kingdom of heaven." *Matthew 19:14*

OBJECT: Two of the children.

THRUST: We would not deliberately exclude someone, but sometimes we fail to include a person.

(This can be a very powerful illustration, in that it deals with an aspect of their lives about which children are quite sensitive. Be sure to explain the process to the two with whom you will be working so that they thoroughly understand what is happening, and why, and that it is only an illustration! As the other children come forward, have one helper sit near you, and the other in back of the group and off to one side.)

This morning we are going to do something really special, and I have been looking forward to it for some time. Before we begin, however, there is something I need to do. *(Turn to the helper sitting near you and give her a rather irritated look.)* June, I don't want you in the group this morning, so go sit somewhere else. *(The child should be instructed to remain where she is, but to look down toward the floor as if feeling very sad. Your comment should take the rest of the children totally by surprise. Let the silence hang for a few moments before you continue.)*

Some of you look a little shocked. Why is that? *(You may get a few guarded responses, but don't expect too much.)* Daniel says he never heard me tell someone to go away before. It does seem a rather rude thing to do, doesn't it? (*You still may not get much response, but the children will agree in their heads.*)

In fact, I suspect that none of us would tell someone just to go away—that we didn't want them around. That would not be very thoughtful, and certainly it would hurt their feelings. Do you think my telling June to go away may have hurt her feelings? (*You may begin to draw some tentative response at this point.*) I agree. I think it was a very unkind thing to do. We know that Jesus invited everyone, especially the children, to come and share with him. He really loved children.

Actually June and I just wanted to illustrate something for you. June, come over and sit next to me for a minute. (*This is very important. Even though you have briefed the child as to what will happen, you need to reassure her that you are still good friends. Put your arm around her and let her know she is a special part of what is happening.*)

As we have said, none of us would exclude someone, or make them feel bad on purpose, would we? (*Let the children agree. Several may want to expand on the idea. That will help to make the point later.*) Well, I am glad we all agree that we would not send anyone away. But I have one more question. How do you think people feel when they may want to be a part of what we are doing, and we simply don't notice them? We just get busy doing what we are doing and neglect them. How do you think someone would feel about that? (*Again, the children probably will agree that such exclusion is not good. You might ask them how they feel when they are left out.*)

We all seem to agree. None of us likes to be ignored. But what about Mark over there? (*Point to your other helper who has been sitting alone in back of the group.*) He has been sitting there by himself all the time we have been talking about including people; yet no one has even noticed him. Why is that? (*You may get some interesting answers at this point.*)

We all seem to have some thoughts, but I think we have learned something. None of us would hurt someone's feelings and send them away on purpose, but it really is easy just to get busy and not notice someone. The result is that they feel bad and they are left out. Also, we miss all the things they may have to share with us.

This week, I would like you to be especially aware of people who may be left out or overlooked and make a point of including them in what you are doing. You may make some new friends, and I am sure you will be much happier for doing it.

God Thinks of Everything!

TEXT: He that goes forth weeping, bearing the seed for
            sowing, shall come home with shouts of joy,
            bringing his sheaves with him.   *Psalm 126:6*

OBJECT: A Jack Pine cone. (The talk refers to a Jack Pine
            cone, but any pine cone can be used.)

THRUST: God always provides a way to make things right,
            even after we make a mistake.

I have something with me this morning that really is
fantastic. In fact, you might say it's one of God's great
surprises. *(Hold up the pine cone and see if you get some
rather disappointed looks.)* Some of you don't look very
impressed. Is that because you never thought of pine cones as
being very special? Well, do you know what pine cones do?
*(Some of the children may have some thoughts, and if so, let
them share with the group.)* Darold is pretty close. They
provide seeds for more pine trees. As the seeds grow, the new
trees provide forests for animals to live in, they help conserve
the soil, they provide wood for homes, and all sorts of things.
That does make them pretty important—right? *(Let the
children respond. They may want to add some other things
that trees do.)*

Now with all the great things these pine cones make
possible, what happens if a careless person causes a forest fire
and burns down all those trees? In the process, all the pine
cones and seeds will be burned up, too. Then what? *(The*

children may have some thoughts here, but keep bringing them back to the point that the fire destroys the seeds for new trees that would take the place of the ones that burned.)

With all the seeds burned, it looks pretty hopeless—right? Well, that is why I called this one of God's great surprises. This is called a Jack Pine cone. The interesting thing about it is that in forest fires, it doesn't burn. In fact, this pine cone will release its seeds only after it has been exposed to intense heat, like a forest fire. What do you think of that? God made a special pine cone, just to grow more trees after a fire. That's what I call thinking of everything! (*Let the implications sink in and take full effect.*)

I think one of the other important things we can learn from this is that God also is aware of the fact that we are going to make mistakes, and that he is always ready to forgive us and help us begin again. He continually provides us with the means of starting over and doing a better job.

So the next time you start feeling low or discouraged about some mistake—remember, even if the worst happens, like a huge forest fire, God already has put the seeds for a new start right in the middle of it.

A Time to Grow

TEXT: For everything there is a season, and a time for
          every matter under heaven: a time to be born, and
          a time to die; a time to plant, and a time to pluck
          up what is planted.   *Ecclesiastes 3:1-2*

OBJECT: Three small plant seedlings, and a fourth that is
          much larger than the others. We used young
          tomato plants as they came from the nursery.

THRUST: As Christians, we need nurturing and care and
          time to grow. In accordance with our growth, we
          have different expectations and abilities at
          different times.

I know that some of you have gardens at home, and I have
seen some really great plants growing in them. Do many of
you help with the gardening? Good, it looks as though several
of you do. You may be able to give me some advice about a bit of
a problem I am having.

As you can see, I have one plant here that is growing fairly
well. I started it about three weeks ago, and I watered it and
cared for it and it has grown this much. *(Set one of the smaller
plants in front of you where the children can see it.)* This is the
second plant I started, and I have watered it and cared for it
too. As you can see, it's about the same size as the first one.
(Set it down next to the first.) This is the third one I planted. It
seemed to be doing well, and I watered it every day, also. As
you can see, these three plants are all about the same size and

shape. Now, here is my problem. *(Lift up the fourth plant, which is a great deal larger than the others.)*

Would you believe I did exactly the same thing with this plant that I did with the others? I planted it six weeks ago, watered it, cared for the soil, and gave it plenty of sun—but look at the difference! It doesn't make any sense. *(Some of the children may offer the immediate answer, or they may ask some tentative questions. If so, let the conversation flow until the answer evolves from the children.)*

Brad says he has the answer. What it is? *(Let the child explain. Others may want to add to his thoughts.)* You are telling me that the large plant is older than the first three. Is that all? What about the difference in size and shape and strength of the stem and all those things? There are lots of differences besides age. *(The children usually will enjoy the fun of such a discussion and should join in explaining why the plants are different.)*

I think I understand. You are telling me that the longer the plant grows and is properly cared for, the bigger and stronger it gets. So all the differences I mentioned are only a result of growth and care. I must admit, I think you are right. In fact, it should be sort of obvious. This last one is larger because it has had a longer time to grow.

Now it didn't take us long to figure that out, and if we could talk to one of the first three plants, we could say, "Don't worry about it. You are doing just fine. As you grow and get stronger, you will be doing all the things the bigger plant is doing, and maybe more." *(Make sure the children have thoroughly grasped the fact that the major difference is one of time.)*

I think we can learn something from our plants. Lots of times, when we are young, we begin to feel bad because we can't do some of the things older folks can do. We begin to think we never will be able to do them. Have you ever felt that

45

way? (*Some of the children may have feelings to share at this point.*)

I would like to suggest that from now on, when you find yourself feeling that way, stop and remember our plants. Our first three are good strong plants. The only difference between them and the last plant is that they haven't had as long to grow. Remember—as you grow, you learn and understand more. The important thing is to be sure that you are really doing some growing and learning each day.

This week, whenever you sense that "feel bad" coming on, say to yourself, "I'm learning new things every day and growing stronger as I go." Then thank God for all the things you *can* do, and feel good about what you have accomplished and all the good things to come.

Being Constructive and Being Angry

TEXT: Be angry but do not sin; do not let the sun go down on your anger. *Ephesians 4:26*

OBJECT: Select three pieces of 1 x 12 pine—one piece 12 inches and two pieces 8 inches long—some nails, and a hammer.

THRUST: We all become angry, and it is important that we use that anger in a constructive manner—not in a destructive manner.

I want to share something with you this morning that is really different. I want to share an emotion. Do you know what that word means? (*Let some of the older children give some examples.*) Right! Derrick says emotions are feelings, such as sad, mad, and glad. That is very good.

The emotion I want to share this morning is *anger.* Sometimes I find myself getting angry about some particular thing. Do any of you ever feel angry? (*Let them relate some experiences.*)

Well, that's how I feel this morning. I have found that when I'm angry, I want to be doing something. So I have decided to hit this board with a hammer. That may help to burn up some of my frustration. (*Lay the end of the 12-inch piece at a right angle to the end of the 8-inch piece so that the 8-inch piece becomes a leg between the floor and the 12-inch piece.*) Kristin, if you will hold this end, I will drive some nails in this board. (*Fasten the two pieces. Then nail the other 8-inch leg to the other end of the 12-inch board. You should have three sides of a square.)*

There, now I feel a little better. Do you know what I did? Mike says I pounded nails. That's right. But do you know what else I did? *(Some of the children may guess. Some of them may figure it out.)* Linda knows. I made a little step stool to stand on when I want to reach a high place. In other words, I was angry, and I wanted to do something, so I did something positive. I pounded nails, but I built something in the process. That's really what I wanted to suggest to you this morning.

Many times we feel that anger is wrong and that we shouldn't feel the way we do. I'm not so sure about that. We know that there are some things we ought to be angry about. Jesus was angry. He was angry about the way some people were treated. The real question is this: What do we do with our anger? Do we use it to destroy, or to build? I could have used the hammer to break things, but I used it to build. I still got rid of my frustration, and I have something positive to show for it.

This week, when you feel yourself becoming angry, ask yourself what you can do with all that energy that will be positive. Then go ahead and do it! That way, when the anger is gone, you can feel good about something you have created from it.

Which Would You Choose?

TEXT: Why do you spend your money for that which is
            not bread, and your labor for that which does not
            satisfy? Hearken diligently to me, and eat what is
            good, and delight yourselves in fatness. Incline
            your ear, and come to me; hear, that your soul
            may live.   *Isaiah 55:2-3*

OBJECT: A handful of coins of all denominations, and a
            tray.

THRUST: Just as some coins are worth more than others, so
            some ideas are of greater value than others.

This morning I am going to ask some of you if you will make some decisions for us. I have some things that I am going to put on this tray, and I would like you to tell me which ones you would take. *(Spread a number of coins out on the tray.)*

Jerimy, if you could pick any three coins, which ones would you take? *(Be sure to ask children who are aware of the differences in monetary amounts.)* That was quite a choice. Out of all those coins, he picked three fifty-cent pieces. Why do you think he selected those? *(Let the children explain the reasons to some of the younger ones who may not know.)*

I think I understand his reason. Let's mix his coins back in and see what someone else would choose. Dustin, if you could select any three, which would they be? Fascinating! *He choose the very same three!* Will you tell us why?

Well, we know that Jerimy and Dustin chose the ones that

49

are most valuable. I guess that is a logical choice. In fact, I think all of us would do the same thing. When we are given a choice, we select the one that is best for us. At least that is what we are saying. But I would like to take a moment to think about some other selections.

Most of us probably have a large number of television programs to choose from, just as we had a large number of coins. Do you choose the one that is the most valuable, or do you just pick one at random? We may ask the same question about books. With all we have to choose from, which ones do we select to read? The very best, or just whatever? It is important, because what we select will determine what we gain from the experience.

This week, when you are planning to do or read or watch something, I would like you to pause for a moment and remember these coins. Then ask yourself if what you are doing or reading or watching is really the very best selection you can make, or if you are choosing pennies and missing something more valuable.

There are only so many things we can do in a day, so let's make those things the very best we can choose.

Would You Like
the Recipe?

TEXT: The Beatitudes. *Matthew 5:2-12*

OBJECT: A recipe card.

THRUST: God has given us the recipe for a wonderful life; all we have to do is follow it.

I have a three-by-five card with me that is a really wonderful thing to have. Can you guess why? (*You may get some ideas, but don't spend too much time with it at this point.*) No, you haven't got it yet. Let me tell you how I got the card, and that may help.

I was at a dinner a few weeks ago, and when it was over, the people served the most fantastic cake I have eaten in my entire life. It was unbelievable! When I finished eating, I looked for the man who baked it and asked if I could have the recipe. Now can you guess why this card is important? Right. David got it right off. It is the recipe. If I follow it, then I can enjoy the same fantastic cake again and again, whenever I want. How does that sound to you? (*The children usually can identify with dessert with no difficulty at all!*)

Now, I think what I did was a pretty normal thing. I experienced something that was very good—the cake. Then I thought I would like to have more of it, so I went to the one who knew how to put it together and asked how to do it. Does that sound logical to you? (*The children should have no problem staying with the thought or making the transfer.*) Patti agrees, and everyone else seems to think so, too. It is only

51

logical that if someone has the very best, that person would be the one to go to for the recipe.

In fact, that is why we spend so much time talking about Jesus, or retelling the things he taught. Being with Jesus is a lot like going to that dinner. When we get to know him, we discover that he offers the very best kind of life. He says that he came to give us a life that is full—right to the top! When we see that life offered, it is as if we were looking at the cake—we begin asking for the recipe. How do we put it together so we can have the same kind of life? Do you know what Jesus did? He left us the recipe! We can find it in lots of places in the Bible, but I would like you to look at one special place. It is called the Beatitudes. Sit down with your parents tonight and read it, thinking of it as a recipe for living a Christian life of joy and service. Talk about what it means and about how you can follow it in your daily actions, and see what happens. God's promise is that you will have the most fantastic life you could possibly imagine.

But What Does That Have to Do with It?

TEXT: A man of quick temper acts foolishly, but a man of
          discretion is patient.   *Proberbs 14:17*

OBJECT: A can of paint and a paint brush.

THRUST: When things go wrong and we have a bad day, we
          frequently strike out at others, as if making them
          feel bad, too, will solve our problem.

Last week a friend of mine came over to the house to ask if
I would help him solve a problem. He was having trouble
with his car, and he knew that I had just finished taking a
course in auto repair. He pulled the car into the driveway,
and we listened to the engine for a few minutes, and he was
right. He did indeed have something wrong with his car. The
engine had a terrible knock. It just did not sound right at all.
Have any of you ever worked on cars? *(Some of the children
may be "helpers" and will take great pride in telling all the
things they can do. Let them enjoy it.)*

From what some of you have said, you already may have a
good idea about how I fixed it. When I heard the knock I told
my friend not to worry. I could solve it with no trouble at all.
Do you know what I used? *(There may be several guesses; let
them run the full gamut.)* I used this. *(Hold up the paint
brush and can. It should draw some rather blank expressions and possibly a few comments.)*

Some of you look as if you don't have much confidence in

this tool, but I will explain. His car had a knock in the engine. Now, as I thought about it, I realized that I never had seen a red car with racing stripes with a knock in its engine. Therefore, if red cars with racing stripes do not have knocks, the solution is simple. Just paint his car red and put on some racing stripes; then the knock will go away. That should fix everything.

Patti, what are you laughing about? It makes perfect sense to me. *(Let the children point out the problem and expand on it in detail.)*

All right, let me make sure I understand you. You are saying that painting the outside of the car has nothing to do with how the inside works? Do the rest of you feel that way? *(Let them all join in.)*

I must agree. It really is a silly solution. In fact, as you pointed out, the so-called solution was not a solution at all. It was completely inappropriate.

I would like you to think, for the next few moments, about another completely inappropriate solution, but this is one lots of people try to use. It goes like this. I am having a really bad day. Everything seems to go wrong, and I am really upset. Have any of you ever had a day like that? I thought so. Well, here is what lots of people do: They jump on someone else and really are grouchy with them. Would that solve the problem and make me feel better?

Nikki, why are you shaking your head? You don't think that's the answer? It would be like painting a car to fix the engine . . . a totally wrong response. Well, I think you are correct. But if jumping on others is not the answer, what is? *(The children may have some good input at this point.)* Daniel seems to have a good idea. Go off by ourselves and ask God to help us get it together. David says we should calm down and think about how Jesus would handle it. I think you

54

have a lot of good ideas. This week, let's put those ideas into practice and not spread our "bad days" around. Let's handle them in an appropriate manner by dealing with the real problems and by getting help from God to solve those problems.

What Did He Say?

TEXT: And as your servant was busy here and there, he was gone. *I Kings 20:40*

OBJECT: The children.

THRUST: We frequently get so busy with our own conversations and activities that we drown out God's attempts to speak to us.

This morning I would like several of you to help me, if you will. *(There should be a number of volunteers without any further urging.)* Oh, that's great! Would you believe I have a job for every one of you? I would like each of you to turn to the person next to you and talk for a few moments. If you can't think of anything to say, that's all right; just tell them your name, your birthday, and your favorite food. Go ahead and visit, and I will just sit here for a while. *(If the children hesitate, you may want to turn to one of them close to you and set the example. Make sure your conversation is on a one-to-one basis, however, or the rest of the children may simply sit and listen.)*

(Let the children have time to really get into their subjects; then, VERY softly say, "I really like you, Mark. And I think Nikki is really nice." *Make the comments softly and very casually. At best, only a few of the children will be aware of the fact that you are talking. After a moment, you may resume in a normal tone.)*

Tammy, I noticed that you stopped talking. Why? *(She may say she thought you said something.)* Tammy thinks she heard me say something. Did any of the rest of you hear anything? Well, a few of you did, but most of you did not. Jimmy heard something, but he didn't understand it. What do you think was happening just now?

Johnny seems to have a good explanation. He says all of you were having your own conversations and didn't hear what I said. Would the rest of you agree with that? Right. That is exactly what happened, isn't it?

I asked you to do this with me this morning for a reason. Many times we do with God the same thing we just did here. We become very busy with our own actions and with living our own lives, and we don't take any time out to listen quietly for what God may say. He may be there, saying very important things, but we just drown him out with our hurry and our noise. We get busy, and we miss what he has to say.

This week, I would like you to do something very special. I would like you to take just a few moments when you first wake up, just as your left eye opens. *(The children have fun with instructions like that, and they will remember them much longer.)* Then listen with your mind and with your heart. See if you can feel God near you. Then go about the rest of the day, knowing he is there.

Then at night, as you are falling asleep, do it again. Lie quietly and thank him for being with you all day. Feel what he is saying to you as you fall asleep. Then when we come together next week, we may want to share how close God is to us and how good we felt when we were quiet enough to listen and hear what he said.

Green Lemonade!?!?

TEXT: Now we, brethren, like Isaac, are children of promise. *Galatians 4:18*

OBJECT: Lemonade in a tall clear glass, so it will be easy for the children to see what happens when you drop in an ice cube that has been colored a dark blue with food coloring. Heighten the color of the lemonade with a touch of yellow food coloring so the results will be more striking. A spoon will be necessary to stir as the ice cube melts. Drop the cube in soon after you begin the talk, in order to give it some time to start changing the color of the lemonade to green.

THRUST: Our nationality, skin color, or sex does not make us any different from one another. Just as the lemonade, even though it is a different color, is still lemonade, so are we, on the inside, all alike. We are all God's children, and it does not make any difference what color we are.

I have one of my favorite drinks with me this morning—*lemonade!* I can see already that some of you must like it, too. Is that right? I thought so. As you can see, this is made with the real thing. It is even a pretty golden yellow color. *(With the extra drop of yellow food coloring and the clear glass, it should be very inviting.)*

Would one of you like to taste it? It really is good. *(If possible, select a volunteer whom you feel will balk at the color change.)* We have a number of helpers. Mark, will you move a little closer so everyone can see you? *(Begin to hand him the glass, then take it back.)* I almost forgot. Warm lemonade is not always the best. Let me put an ice cube in and stir it around a little. *(Pick up the dark blue cube slowly, so that several of the children will have an opportunity to see it and comment on it. One negative response will start the ball rolling. Drop the cube in the warm lemonade and begin to stir.)*

This will cool it off; then it will taste better. Heather, what are you wrinkling your nose about? *(Let the children respond directly to the blue ice cube. As they talk, someone will notice that the lemonade is beginning to change color. That will draw comment, as well.)*

Candace says the ice cube looked weird. What do some of the rest of you think? *(Let them respond.)* Well, it was dark blue, and I must admit, I haven't seen a lot of dark blue ice cubes. But I'm sure it will be fine.

Now Lance says the lemonade is changing color. *(Hold up the glass.)* You're right. It really is. It's turning green. I guess the blue and the yellow are combining to make it look green. What do you think about that? *(You will probably get a variety of responses.)* Mark says he's not too sure he wants to drink it. It looks different. Do you agree? Well, it is a different color—a very pretty green. I wonder if it's still lemonade. Do you think it is? *(You may get a variety of responses, since several of the younger children will reason that if it is a different color, it has to be different.)*

Well, we seem to have several ideas. There is one sure way to check. Mark, will you taste it and tell us? *(Let him taste and respond.)* It's good! It is still lemonade, even though it is a different color. How about that! The color didn't make any difference at all! It is the inside—the flavor—that is really important. This lemonade has a pretty color that is different

59

from the lemonade we usually see, but it is still lemonade. It is not the color that's important.

We can learn a real lesson from our glass of lemonade. Sometimes we make the same mistake with people that we almost made with our lemonade. We think that if someone is a different color, then they must be different. The important thing, however, is not the color, but what is inside.

As Christians, we know that God made everyone and that his Spirit is inside each person. It is not the color that counts, but the Spirit. This week, let's look deeper into the people we meet. Let's go beyond the color, or outward appearance, and see the special gifts God has given them to share in his Spirit. Then we will know what they are really like.

Help That Lasts

TEXT: I can do all things in him who strengthens
          me. *Philippians 4:13*

OBJECT: A barbell or some other type of weight that can be
          lifted with one hand.

THRUST: God frequently answers our prayer for help by
          giving us the strength to overcome our problems.

I have something with me this morning that I work with on
a regular basis. I'm sure several of you know what it is, and
some of you may have worked with one. *(Let some of the older
children describe it and relate its purpose to the others.)*

Daniel knows; it's a weight, and people use them to firm up
or strengthen their muscles. If that is the case, what do you
think would happen to my arm if I spent a lot of time every day
doing this? *(Do some simple curls with the weight as you talk.)*

Right! Patti says the arm would become stronger. Why?
*(Several of the children may know why and how a muscle
develops, so don't be too quick to help them with the answer.)*

David says the muscle has to work to lift the weight, and the
more it has to work, the stronger it gets. Is that what the rest of
you think? *(Let some of the others share with their insights.)*

If what you say is correct, and I believe it is, what would
happen to this same arm if I said I wanted to protect it and be
nice to it, and I just tied it up in a sling? That way it would
never have to work or strain with anything, ever again. What
would happen to it? *(It may take a second, but the children*

will make the connection, and when they do, it will be their discovery and help them in relating it to other things.)

Jennifer doesn't seem to think that would be very helpful. She says the arm would get weaker and weaker. Jennifer, I believe you are correct.

Now, here is what I would like you to think about. What is true of our arm is also true of several other things, including our spiritual growth and strength. There are times when all of us face real problems, and our tendency is to pray for God to jump in and take care of us—sort of put us in a sling and carry us for a while. Sometimes God may do that, but I think most of the time we get a different type of answer. Can any of you tell me what it might be? *(You may receive some very insightful responses at this point. You also may gain a great deal of personal insight as to how the children are shaping their understanding of what God is all about.)*

Richard says that if we have to work through the problem ourselves, we will become stronger and be able to do more. I think that's right. God promises to be with us and to help us, and with that strength, we can grow and do all sorts of things.

This week, when we ask God to remove some problem, and the problem does not go away, let's accept that as an invitation to grow—to make use of the strength God will give us to overcome whatever faces us.

It's Only a Little Tree

TEXT: And the King will answer them, "Truly I say to you, as you did it to one of the least of these my brethren, you did it to me." *Matthew 25:40*

OBJECT: An ax handle.

THRUST: Everyone is important, and when we treat one person as if he or she is not, everyone's value decreases.

I heard a very interesting story a long time ago, from my grandfather, and I would like to share it with you. It is about a man who went into the woods to get a tree. The first tree he picked was the tallest, straightest one, and he said, "I'll take this one."

Well, you can imagine how surprised he was when he heard a deep voice say, "No you won't!" Who do you think said it? *(Asking periodic questions is a good way to keep the children with the story and also to make sure you haven't confused anyone.)*

No, it wasn't God—it was the tree! It said, "I am the king of these trees. You can't take me; I'm too important." The man thought about that and then decided he would take one a little farther away. But the trees said he couldn't have that one, either. It was an important member of the tree council.

That kind of discussion went on for some time, and finally the man settled on a solution. Can you guess what it was? *(Let them have several tries—it will not break the story line at this*

63

point.) Some of you are pretty close. He said the trees could select among themselves which one he would have. That seemed fair enough.

Well, the trees went into a very deep discussion. They thought of one tree and then another, but each one seemed to be too important.

Then they found the answer. Way off on the edge of the forest was a little tiny tree that wasn't more than five feet high. It hadn't produced any fruit or nuts yet, and it was too small to offer any shade. It didn't do much of anything, except stand there. They all agreed. That was the one tree of no importance. They could give it up, and it would make no difference. What do you think about that? (*Allow plenty of time for answers and rationale.*)

We seem to have some mixed thoughts, so let me tell you what happened. The man thanked the trees and went and pulled up the little one, and he shaped it into one of these. (*Hold up the ax handle.*) Do you know what this is? (*Some of the children may know and figure out the point of the story immediately. If so, let them have the fun of explaining.*)

Jason has it figured out exactly. The man took the tree that the others had felt was unimportant, and he used it to make a handle for his ax. Then, with a new ax, he was able to cut down even the biggest trees. Do you think there might be a message in that for us? (*This is a great time, in that the children are free to make the connection and application. It helps you discover if you are getting too abstract, or if they are thinking along the same lines.*)

I think most of us have come to similar conclusions. Everyone is important, and whenever we treat someone as if he or she is not, it is a bad thing for all of us. Remember that this week, while you are at school or playing. Take time to include everyone, and treat each one as an important person. All people are God's children and that makes everyone *very* special!

So Much for That!

TEXT: You are the salt of the earth; but if salt has lost its taste, how shall its saltness be restored? It is no longer good for anything except to be thrown out and trodden under foot by men.   *Matthew 5:13*

OBJECT: A dried-up felt-tip pen and a drawing tablet.

THRUST: We are called to a purpose, and if we do not follow that purpose, great opportunities frequently are missed.

This morning I have a really great picture to share with you. It not only has a good thought, but it is one of the funniest pictures I ever have learned to draw. Every time I draw it, I just sit and laugh. If you all will gather around, I'll show you. *(Have the children come in close, turn to a clean sheet of drawing paper and then pull out your pen.)*

Now watch carefully; this is great. *(Make two or three broad strokes with the dried-up pen. You will be leaving no marks on the paper.)* What is this? *(Some of the children may be calling it to your attention already.)* I don't believe this. The pen doesn't work! *(Stop and look at it carefully.)* The tip is all dried up. Well, I guess that is the end of that! *(It may take a moment for it to register. Then you will get some comment.)*

I agree. It really is disappointing when you are depending on something to help you do an important job, and then you discover it will not work. *(Let the children add a few more comments.)* There is really nothing left to do with the pen but throw it out.

I think we can learn an important lesson from this experience, however. Do you remember that once when Jesus was talking, he said that Christians are like the salt of the earth? Now salt is used for lots of very special things, and it is very important. In fact, salt used to be one of the most important things around.

But then Jesus added, "If the salt has lost the qualities that make it salty, what good is it? You might as well toss it out. It won't do the job." He is telling us something very important. We are like the pen or the salt. As Christians, there are many special and important things we are called to do, and we are the only ones who can do some of them. So God depends on us, just as we were depending on the pen. If we do what the pen did, God's program is stopped for awhile, and he has to try another way. I don't think God will throw us out, because he loves us too much. But he will have to start all over again; we will have missed a chance to help, and there may be a very important job that didn't get done.

This week, let's be the very best we can be, and do all the things God has for us to do.

Still Getting the Best

TEXT: We know that in everything God works for good with those who love him, who are called according to his purpose. *Romans 8:28*

OBJECT: One drawing paper and a felt-tip pen.

THRUST: Many of us have different types of handicaps or problems, but if we open our lives to God, he still can work through us and bring out the very best in us.

(To prepare for this talk it would be helpful to get a basic book on drawing flowers from the public library. If you have some natural talent, that is great. Those of us who do not, can pick up enough pointers to get by, with a little practice.)

This morning, I want to show you something I learned to draw. It will take a while, because it is a seascape and has a sailing ship in it, with lots of ropes and lines to get in the right places. *(As you set up your drawing tablet, let your pen "slip" and run a long wide stripe over half way down the center of the page.)*

Oh no! I don't believe I did that. I just ruined a perfectly good piece of paper. To make it worse, that was my last one. Now I am not sure what to do with our time. I was going to draw a ship, but there is no way to get a ship to go in with that ink smear. I don't know about you, but I find it very discouraging. Have any of you ever had anything like that happen to you? *(Several of the children may have had experiences so similar that they can truly identify.)*

Well, I'll tell you what I think I am going to do. I have been looking at that nasty line down the middle of the paper. It really does ruin the ship I had in mind, but I think it might make a great stem for a flower—especially a rose. What do some of you think? *(You may get a number of suggestions.)*

I think David is right. Instead of throwing it away, I will show you how to draw a rose. *(Using simple techniques from the drawing book, you can produce a very attractive rose, or flower of your choice.)* There. I think it looks pretty good. *(You should do as well as you can. Quality IS part of the point.)*

Nikki says she likes it and so does Daniel. You know, I think there may be a very important lesson in this. We started out wanting a ship. Then we hit two real problems. First we messed up the paper; then we discovered that there was no more paper. Now at that point we could have thrown up our hands and given up. We never could have our ship, so all was hopeless. Have you ever been tempted to react to disappointment that way? *(The children may want to share some deeper feelings at this point.)*

Well, Patti is right. At some times, all of us feel like that. In a sense, those are very important times in our life. They are the times when we decide if we simply are going to give up, or if we will press on and do the best we can. We may not always get our first choice, but we still can do some great things.

You remember that the apostle Paul was running into problems constantly. He was frequently forced to change his plans, yet in the end, he did a tremendous work. I think the same is true for us.

When you become discouraged, that is the time to say, "I may not get my first choice, or do it the first time, but I know that God can show me a way to bring something good out of this." Then get busy and see what you and God can do.

Nobody Knew . . . Almost

TEXT: Better is a poor man who walks in his integrity
          than a rich man who is perverse in his ways.
          Proverbs 28:6

OBJECT: Some cookies on a plate.

THRUST: We feel better about ourselves when we have
          done what we know is right.

I have these cookies with me because some other cookies just like these helped me to learn a very important lesson, and I would like to share it with you.

When I was younger, I loved cookies more than anything. They were my favorite food. Do you like cookies? Good; then you all know how I felt about them.

One day my mother had baked some cookies, and they came out of the oven just before dinner. She said we were going to serve them to some people coming over later that evening and that I shouldn't eat any right then. It was too close to supper, and besides, I could have some later. Have you ever been in a situation like that? *(The children should have no trouble at all identifying.)*

Well, I don't know how *you* handled it, but I'll tell you what I did. I looked at those cookies and looked at them, and I could almost hear them talking to me. They were saying, "Go ahead and take one; no one will ever know." Have you ever heard a cookie say that? *(You may get several responses from a wide range of personal experiences.)*

I am sure that you know as well as I do that cookies can't talk, and it was just that I wanted one. So I waited for awhile; then I went over very quietly and took about four cookies and made for the backyard. Then I sat down and ate them all.

Can you guess what my mother said when I went back in? *(This question can lead to some very insightful comments also.)* No, she wasn't angry. No, she didn't say it was all right. In fact, she didn't say anything, because she never knew. No one in the whole world knew . . . except me! That is when I made my discovery. I didn't feel very good about it. A person I loved had trusted me, and I did something I shouldn't have done. Maybe you have known someone who has been in that situation. *(By shifting the problem to an unnamed third party it is made less threatening, and the children can deal with it openly.)*

It really left me with a bad feeling. Doug says he has done some things he didn't feel very good about afterward. In fact, I think everyone in the whole world has. It is part of learning and growing. The important thing is what we do about it.

What I did was learn a lesson. I said to myself right there, that from now on, whenever I begin to do something, I am going to stop and say, I want to do this now, but how will I feel about myself later on? How will I feel if other people know I have done it? If I decide I will feel bad, then that is a pretty good sign I shouldn't do it.

This week, try that system, and see if it works for you.

Watch the Watch!

TEXT: Do your best to present yourself to God as one
          approved, a workman who has no need to be
          ashamed, rightly handling the word of truth.
          II Timothy 2:15

OBJECT: A watch or clock—the more ornate it is, the more
          the children will be inclined to study it.

THRUST: If the Scripture or anything else is going to fulfill
          its purpose, we must use it the way its creator
          intended it to be used, and not according to any
          mistaken ideas of our own.

*(I have found that a clock can be a very good object for
conveying this message. Even the youngest child knows it has
a specific and important purpose; yet most of them are unable
to tell time and feel a certain frustration about that inability.)*

This morning I have something that I know all of you will
recognize. It is a clock, and it was made in Switzerland. If you
look closely, you can see all the little figures painted on it. It
really is a very pretty clock. *(Let the children get a good look at
it and allow them time to comment. Some of them may want to
tell you about their watches or clocks. If so, let them share. Not
only is this important to them, but it will help to bring out the
point of the conversation.)*

I see from the comments that several of you have clocks or
watches of your own. That's really great. I guess most of you
know what clocks are for then. *(You should get a general*

71

response concerning the telling of time. This is a real issue for youngsters.)

Now wait a minute. I hear all of you talking about the same thing—telling time. *(Allow a few moments for the children to confirm that.)* Well, that may be so, but I have lots of other uses for my clock. As you can see, it's attractive, so I use it mostly as a decoration. I set it somewhere in the house so people can look at it and say, "What a pretty clock." *(At this point some of the children may point out that that is not the purpose of a clock. If so, let them make their point.)*

Karla seems to feel that even if a clock is pretty, it still ought to be used to tell the time. Is that right? I thought that's what you meant. In that case, you probably would not approve of some of my other uses for the clock. In meetings I use it as a gavel to get people's attention. I just thump it on the table a few times and people stop talking. I see some of you don't think that's the best idea. *(Allow for comments.)*

Well, other times I have tossed it to someone to get their attention. Is that better? No? I thought not. I could use it to get spare parts for other clocks, but I guess that is not what you had in mind, either. Well, you will be glad to know that I usually wind it and let it run like it is now. Does that make you feel better? *(Let the children respond to the proper use of the clock. Some of the older ones may notice that the time is wrong. If not, you can introduce the idea yourself.)*

I just wind it up, like it is now. It says it is three o'clock. What? *(You should get a response.)* Kyle says that's not right either. You mean there is more to it than just winding it? I have to set it and then learn to read it properly? I think I begin to see your point.

You are telling me that the clock was made for a specific purpose and meant to be used in a certain way. As I have said, there are lots of other ways I could use it, but none of them are the way the creator of the clock intended it to be used. Right? I thought so. You are telling me I must put some effort into learning to read the hands on the clock so that I can get the full benefit from it, and not just make guesses. Well, I think you are absolutely correct.

I also believe there is a very important lesson we can learn from our discussion. What is true about a clock is true also about the Bible. We can use it for a lot of different things. It can be a decoration on a coffee table, but never opened. It can be a paperweight. It even can be read but misunderstood, because we did not prepare ourselves. That would be like winding the clock but not setting the hands and not knowing how to tell time. To use the clock properly, we must make some preparation, just as to read the Bible, we must prepare ourselves properly.

What I am suggesting is that God has given us a great gift in the Bible, but like a watch or a clock, we need to learn the right way to use it and read it before we can get the full benefit from it.

When your parents read your Bible with you, take some time to be sure you know the meaning of all the words. See how the ideas can be used every day in what you do or feel. Then as you learn more and more about who wrote the Bible and about what they were really saying, you will be able to understand God's message more completely.

Who Can Write
the Biggest Number?

TEXT: In Christ God was reconciling the world to himself, not counting the people's trespasses against them, and entrusting to us the message of reconciliation. *II Corinthians 5:19*

OBJECT: A chalk board and chalk.

THRUST: God is so big, there is no way we can ever grasp all of him; yet as big as he is, he loves *you!*

This morning I would like to have a contest. Would some of you be willing to enter it? Good—we have a lot of helpers with us. This is a great contest because everyone can take part. Daniel, will you please write a big number on the chalk board for us? (*Many of the children are just learning to count, and others will be feeling fairly comfortable with numbers. Usually a three or four digit number is considered "big."*)

Very good. Daniel wrote the number 343. That's a pretty big one, isn't it? There are only a few more days than that in an entire year. Now, can anyone write a number larger than that one? David says he can. What will you write for us? Very Good. David's number, 670, really is bigger, isn't it? Almost twice as big, in fact. Ronnie says he knows a really big one. Wow! —729,130! That really is a big one. How many of you have ever seen a number that big? Some of you have. (*Let the children have some fun with it and continue to add larger numbers. Be aware when the younger ones begin to lose interest, however. Numbers are new to them and as they*

74

become larger, the smaller children may be impressed, but they can't hold the concept.)

You know, I get the feeling we could go on like this for a long time. Do any of the rest of you feel that way? The fact is, there is no such thing as "the biggest number." No matter how big a number we write, someone always could put another number in front of it, and that would make it bigger. *(You may want to illustrate this as you say it. Use smaller numbers again, so the younger ones can relate to them. You may use a 7; then add a 1, for 17; then another 1, for 117. That should make the point without confusing the younger ones.)*

Now, the real reason we are doing this is to show you how big God is. God is a little like that number. No matter how much we learn about him, there is always more. God always has been here, and he will be here forever. Like some of the numbers we mentioned, that's bigger and longer than we ever could imagine. That's why learning about God and coming to know some things about him is so important.

But God knows that we have a hard time understanding things that big. Did some of you have trouble with the number 1742396114628372146? Boy, I sure did! I not only don't know how much it is, I can't even say it! Sometimes we are that way with God. He is so great, we can't even imagine what he is like. So do you know what he did to help us? Right! Mary Carol knows. He sent Jesus in the form of a person. That's why Jesus is so important. In him, we see what God is really like, in a way we can understand.

And I'll tell you one more way that God is like our number. You remember we said it is impossible to write the biggest number because there is always another number that can be added to it? Well, Jesus told us that the same is true of God's love. No matter how much we think there is, there is always more, waiting to be given to us. Look at this. *(Write a number from one side of the board to the other.)* That is a fantastic

75

number, isn't it? But that's not even a little bit of how big God is, and it isn't even a start on how much he loves you.

This week, look up at all the stars and think about how big God is, and remember—he loves you a million times more than all the stars you can count. That's really a lot!

How People Say "Thank You"

TEXT: And out of pity for him the lord of that servant
          released him and forgave him the debt. But that
          same servant, as he went out, came upon one
          of his fellow servants who owed him . . . and
          seizing him by the throat he said, "Pay what you
          owe." *Matthew 18:27-28*

OBJECT: A two-foot-square piece of poster board, with the
          words THANK YOU written in five or six different
          languages.

THRUST: There are many ways to say thank you—some-
          times with words, but most effectively, with
          actions.

I have a poster with me this morning that is being used in
Nikki's Brownie troop, and I would like to share it with you.
*(Any time you can use an object that was made by or belongs
to one of the children, it strengthens the point of contact.)*
   As you can see, there are a lot of words on it. Can anyone tell
me what they mean? *(You will get some interesting guesses
that may give you an insight into where the children think
YOU are. What kind of words would they expect you to select?
It is also an excellent opportunity if you have some children
who can read or speak a second language. Be sure to include
their "speciality.")*
   We have some good guesses, but no one has gotten it yet.
Nikki, possibly you or Kristin would be willing to enlighten us.

(If you don't have this type of situation, simply go through the list and let the children repeat the words and learn some of them. At this age, foreign languages are a fascination.)

I think you got the whole list: *obrigado* in Portuguese, *muchas gracias* in Spanish, *danke* in German, *merci* in French, *arigato* in Japanese, *eucharisto soi* in Greek, and *todah* in Hebrew. *(The last three are more effective and fun if written in the characters of those languages.)*

That is quite a list, and you all did a good job pronouncing them. Now you have learned several ways to say thank you. It really is a very important phrase.

I would like to talk for just a moment about another way to say thank you that is somewhat different. Let's say I always had wanted to play the piano, and one day my parents bought one for me. What could I say? *(Let the children have some fun, in that they may want to try out their new words.)* Those are good expressions. Now let's go one step further. What do you think my parents might think if, after saying all those thank yous, I never bothered to play the piano? *(The children will be able to identify with that rather easily.)*

I think you all get the idea. It is important to *say* thank you with words, but it is also important to say it with *actions*. In fact, that is the best way to say thank you to God. It is important to thank God through prayer and worship, but the best way is to take his love that we have received and share it with others. When we accept the gifts we have and use them for others, we are actually *doing* our thank you!

This week, let's see how many ways we can *do* a thank you with our actions.

Getting to Know You

TEXT: And [Peter] said to them, "You yourselves know
           how unlawful it is for a Jew to associate with or to
           visit any one of another nation; but God has
           shown me that I should not call any man common
           or unclean. *Acts 10:28-29*

OBJECT: A large bag of candy.

THRUST: Prejudice not only is unfair; it is not Christ-like.

This morning I was a little concerned that we might not
have enough candy to go around, but I can see now that we do.
I have about fifteen pieces here. *(Select a number that is
roughly half the number of the children in your group. Some of
them will notice this immediately; the others will catch on as
things progress.)*

To make it easier to hand out the candy, I would like all of
you with blue eyes to hold up your hands. That's good. If you
will keep them raised for a few minutes it will help me,
because I will know who does not like candy. *(That should
draw a number of comments, and several of the hands will go
down.)*

Wait a minute. Some of you are putting your hands down.
You need to keep them raised so you will not get any candy.
*(Let the protests continue for awhile. They will help to make
the point in a very graphic manner.)* June, what is the
problem? Why did you put your hand down? *(Let the children
do the explaining.)*

I don't understand this. Are you telling me you *like* candy? Well, I know for a fact that you are trying to tease me. Someone told me just the other day that people with blue eyes do not like candy. It's a well-known fact! If you have blue eyes you do not like candy. (*Let them give a full response. Some of them may have begun to learn the difference between fact and opinion in school. If so, make the most of it.*)

All right. I guess you have convinced me. You really do like candy. In fact, it is kind of silly to say people would or would not like something just because their eyes are a certain color, isn't it?

I really would like you to remember this talk, because you will hear things like that again in other places. The words may be a little different, but the idea will be the same. It may be said this way: "All black people are . . . "; or you may be told that all girls feel a certain way about something; or that boys can't do something just because they are boys; or, "All white people are . . . "; the list goes on and on. We call it prejudice when people make a decision about others because of their color or sex or nationality or size, rather than looking at them as individual children of God.

Jesus has a way of looking at us as if each of us is one of a kind. He sees us as individuals and helps us be the very best persons we can be. As followers of Jesus, that is the way we should look at people, too.

This week, let's not make sweeping generalizations about people. Let's get to know them individually and find out what special gifts God has given them.

Drop in Anytime!

TEXT: But as for me, my prayer is to thee, O Lord. At an
         acceptable time, O God, in the abundance of thy
         steadfast love answer me. With thy faithful help
         rescue me from sinking in the mire; let me be
         delivered from my enemies.   *Psalm 69:13*

OBJECT: Two or three appointment cards.

THRUST: We can approach God anytime in prayer, and we
          will be received.

I have something this morning that some of you may have
seen when you went to the doctor or dentist. They are called
appointment cards. Do some of you know what an appointment is? (*Let some of the older children fill in the younger
ones.*) Right! It is a kind of meeting. When we want to see the
doctor we call, and the receptionist finds an open time in the
day, such as three o'clock, and tells us we can come then. That
is our appointment. Why do you think we have to make
appointments with people? (*The children may come up with a
variety of reasons; let them develop each.*)

It sounds as though there are all sorts of reasons for making
appointments, but what I heard coming through was that the
people we are wanting to see are very busy, and there are only
certain times when they will be free to see us. Sometimes it may
be several days before we can get in for a visit. Have any of you
ever had that experience? (*Let the children share freely. They
enjoy sharing experiences and feel good about being included.*)

People really are busy aren't they? Have you ever thought about how busy God must be? Why, he keeps the whole universe running! Everything stays in balance, from the smallest little bugs that can be seen only with a miscroscope, to the biggest stars, so far away we need a telescope to see them. That is a tremendous lot to keep moving. And along with all that there are all the millions of prayers and problems to be handled each day. That really must be a huge work load. *(Get the children agreeing as they contemplate the size of the task being described.)*

Now, what I would like to know is this—with God having all that work, when you want to talk to him, how long do you have to wait for an appointment? *(You may receive some really interesting responses to this question, because it probably never had crossed their minds before.)*

Derry says he never had thought about that. From the sound of it, not many of you did. God is always there—right? When we want to talk we just start praying or talking, and right away we find God there, responding. That's really something to think about. No matter how busy God might be or how many others need to talk to him at the same time, God is always there when we need to talk.

That's a pretty great thing, wouldn't you say? *(Let the children spend some time pondering the implications. They may come up with some interesting insights.)*

This week, when we talk to God, let's begin by saying, "Thank you for being there!" It really would be bad to need God and to have someone say, "God will be able to hear you at four o'clock next Friday."

God is always there. When we start our conversations with him, let's begin by realizing what a great thing that is, and how much he must love us.

Don't Let Others
Limit Your Talents

TEXT: *(You may want to tell the full context as a part of the talk.)* Now Deborah, a prophetess, the wife of Lappidoth, was judging Israel at that time. . . . Barak said to her, "If you will go with me, I will go; but if you will not go with me, I will not go." *Judges 4:4, 8*

OBJECT: A pipe wrench.

THRUST: It is important not to prejudge people or force them into stereotyped sex roles, or any other kinds of roles.

I think one of the greatest talents or skills some folks have is the ability to fix things. That is why I brought this pipe wrench. I have a friend who is a fantastic plumber. No matter what the problem, it can be fixed in no time. New sinks can be put in, new lines run under the house, water heaters replaced —no job is too big or too complicated. A friend like that really is handy to have. This friend is really special; she is my wife. *(Some of the children may register their surprise openly. If not, you may single one out.)*

Leslie, you look surprised. Have you never encountered a lady plumber? *(Several of the children may want to respond at this point.)* It sounds as if some of you have met ladies who could fix lots of things.

I'll tell you something else that is interesting. The man next door is a great cook, and the girl down the street drives a construction truck. They all have certain likes and dislikes, and they are good at what they do. Don't you think it would be a little silly to tell the man next door that he can't cook because he is a man? (*Let the children respond. There will probably be several daddies who cook.*)

Let's look at another side of it. I know a boy who enjoys playing with dolls. He also plays catcher on the baseball team. He is free to do what he enjoys without being pushed into a mold. It's like saying, "Boys don't cry." That's silly. Everybody knows boys cry. It is a perfectly natural thing to do.

Sometimes we get "hung up" on thinking that only certain people can do certain things or feel certain emotions. That's not only silly, it really can be harmful. I knew a boy once who wanted to play the piano, and he was told that men didn't do that. I'm certainly glad no one ever told Bach or Mozart that! And think of all the men you hear singing on the radio!

In fact, I would like for you to give the whole thing a great deal of thought. If God has given you the talent and ability to do something, do it. Don't let someone stop you by saying only girls or only boys do that. You are free in Christ to do all you can do and to be all you can be, so explore all your talents and learn to use each of them to its fullest.

Dull or Bright?

TEXT: Let your light so shine before men, that they may see your good works and give glory to your Father who is in heaven. *Matthew 5:16*

OBJECT: A piece of stained glass that you can hold in your hand so that the children can see it easily, and a flashlight. You may want to have some pictures of famous windows, as well. If stained glass is unavailable, the same thing can be done with thin paper on a film slide.

THRUST: We are beautiful. God created us that way, but if we do not allow the light of Jesus to shine through us, we lose a great deal of our beauty. To be the "prettiest" that we can be, we need the help of our Creator.

We have been looking at some beautiful pieces of stained glass in a class I am taking, and I want to share one with you. I have a small model of a stained-glass window with a very pretty scene in it. If you will look carefully, I'm sure you will enjoy it. *(Hold it up so that your hand is behind it, blocking the light. All they will see is a rather dark piece of glass and a few vague shades of color.)*

I hope all of you can get a good look at it, because it really is very pretty. *(The children will probably let you know fairly quickly that they do not see any of the things you are describing.)* Jason, you don't look very impressed. What's the

85

problem? You only see a dark piece of glass? How about the rest of you? I see. Well, I believe I have a solution to that problem. (*Place the flashlight behind the glass so that the light shines through it.*) How about that? Does that make a difference? (*Let the children get a good look and express any appreciation they may have.*)

It really is very pretty. Have you ever seen any of these pictures of windows? (*Show the children a few of the pictures.*) Some of them tell the whole story of Jesus' life. As you see, they do it in a very beautiful way.

There is one thing, however, that all these windows, from the simplest to the most elaborate, have in common. Can anyone tell me what it is? (*Let them spend some time sharing and comparing. The give-and-take between the children themselves is important.*)

We have named a few things they have in common, but the one I especially had in mind is this: To really show all their beauty, they must have light shining through them. If there is no light, no one can see all the great things they have to offer.

I believe that in a way, we are much like those windows. Each of us has special talents and a kind of beauty inside us, but sometimes we can't seem to get it out, and those looking at us can't see it. The problem is that we are not letting Christ's light and love shine through us. Now, I don't mean that Jesus stands behind us with a big flashlight. I mean that when we use our talents and abilities to do the kinds of things that Jesus did, then people begin to see us in a new way—they see what Jesus can do in our lives when we let him. We become a kind of window to God. Others can see what God is like; they can see it in the beauty of our lives and actions.

This week, spend some time with your mom or dad and talk about the things Jesus did; ask how you can do the same type of thing. Then his light can begin shining through you, and others will see God through the beauty of your window.

Who Made Your Shirt?

TEXT: And the Lord God made for Adam and for his wife
          garments of skins, and clothed them.
          Genesis 3:21

OBJECT: A shirt.

THRUST: God loves us, even though we make mistakes.

As we sit here together, I notice that we are wearing all
kinds and styles of blouses and shirts. There are all shades of
colors and several different patterns. Some look very warm,
and others look like they would be light and cool. I guess the
best part is that they all look very comfortable. Do you all like
what you have on? That's great!

The shirt I have with me is one that my wife made for me,
and it is really my favorite. Have any of you ever watched
someone make a shirt? (*Several of the children may have
parents who sew, and they may help in explaining the
process.*)

We seem to have a great deal of information here about
sewing. As I listen to this, it sounds as though making a shirt
or a blouse would be a real job. I'm sure there is a lot of
measuring and cutting before we even could get to the sewing
part. It seems to me that if you were going to go to all the work
of selecting the material and making a shirt for someone, you
really would have to like them. Who do you know that has
made a shirt or blouse especially for you? (*Let the children*

name the people who may have made one for them. The names probably will be of immediate family or close friends.)

Both Kyle and David said their mothers made shirts for them. Lance says his grandmother made one. It seems to be the kind of thing that is usually done by someone who loves us. *(Let the children confirm the findings.)*

I'll tell you why that interests me. When I was the age some of you are, I began to wonder what God was like, and I began to ask people about it. I got all sorts of answers, but one of them really impressed me. It was a picture of God with a big sword, and he was sending Adam and Eve out of the Garden of Eden. They looked very sad, and God looked very angry and stern. Have any of you ever seen a picture like that? *(You may get some insights as to the image of God held by the children.)*

Let me tell you something very interesting that I discovered about the story of Adam and Eve. Do you know the very first thing that the Bible says happened to them after they left the garden? *(You may get some great guesses here, or someone may know!)* No, nobody has it, so I'll tell you.

The first thing that happened was that they met God. Do you know what God was doing? He was busy making clothes for them so they wouldn't get cold. How about that! *(Let the children respond and reflect on the meaning of the image of God.)* Daniel says that God couldn't have been very angry if he still liked Adam and Eve enough to do that. What do some of the rest of you think? It does seem a little odd, doesn't it? But that is what the Bible tells us, and it is something I think we should always remember.

It is true that we will make mistakes, and we will do things wrong, but even when we do, God always will be looking for ways to love us and to help us get back to a right relationship with him.

This week, if you feel you have done something wrong, or someone tells you that God may not like you, remember Adam and Eve. After they did something wrong, the first thing God did was to get busy loving them again. Never forget how much God loves you and always stay open to his Spirit.

Blending Talents

TEXT: . . . that their hearts may be encouraged as they are knit together in love, to have all the riches of assured understanding and the knowledge of God's mystery, of Christ. *Colossians 2:2*

OBJECT: Some shaved crayons between waxed paper, a board, and a warm iron. When pressed, colors will blend and create interesting patterns.

THRUST: Colors, blended and worked together, multiply the number of shades that can be achieved, just as people, when they work together, can multiply their achievements.

I want to show you something that I learned to do in Vacation Church School. Watch this carefully . . . it is really interesting. *(Take the shavings from a number of crayons and lay them between the two pieces of waxed paper.)*

Well, what do you think of that? Isn't that pretty? *(The response at this point may be insightful, because you obviously have not created anything, and it isn't much in terms of being "pretty.")*

Some of you look as if you are not very sure what it is. You saw how I made it. I took those shavings and mixed them all into a beautiful swirl of color. *(Let them look again at the flakes lying between the papers.)*

As I look at this a little more closely, I think I may see what is bothering you. We don't have a big swirl of color, do we? We have a lot of little pieces just lying there. Is that the problem you see? *(That should draw the response.)*

What do you think we could do to them to make a swirl of color? *(The children may have a number of suggestions. You may try a few, and if someone suggests the answer you intend to use, that can be your springboard.)*

We don't seem to be having much luck. We have tried shaking them, mashing them, and even talking to them. Nothing has worked. Jody says if we could heat them it might help. That may do it! In fact, I have asked one of the adults to bring us a warm iron and a piece of wood so we can try that. *(Set the two pieces of waxed paper with the shavings between them on the board. Set the iron on them and move it in a circular motion so that it will blend the melting shavings together. It will be cool enough to work with as soon as you finish.)*

That really worked! *(Hold it up so the children all can see the color swirl.)* Jody had the idea—we just had to warm them up. Then when they all began coming together, they created a beautiful pattern.

As we think about this, I believe we can learn a very important lesson. When we first put the shavings between the papers, each one was a pretty color. But as long as they all remained separate and didn't blend with any of the others, they didn't look like much.

People are a lot like that. We all have talents and good things inside us, but if we keep them locked up inside, we never become all the things we could be.

If, however, we add a little warmth, such as God's love and concern, and blend what we have, there is no end to what we can do or how many people we can help.

This week, spend some time working with other people. See what happens when you blend your abilities with theirs. It's a great feeling, and I think you'll really enjoy it.

What Will You Write?

TEXT: And he who had received the five talents came forward, bringing five talents more, saying, "Master, you delivered to me five talents; here I have made five talents more." His master said to him, "Well done, good and faithful servant; you have been faithful over a little, I will set you over much; enter into the joy of your master." *Matthew 25:20-21*

OBJECT: Several 8 1/2 x 11 sheets of paper with various things written on them—some serious, some scribbled—and one sheet of blank paper.

THRUST: Each day is like a new sheet of paper. We must decide what will be written on it at the close of the day.

I was at an interesting meeting a few days ago. It was for people who would like to write stories. The leader gave each person a blank sheet of paper and said, "This is your paper. You may do whatever you want with it for the next half hour."

If someone handed you a blank sheet of paper, what would you do? Nikki says she would draw. Ricky would write a story. Kristin would practice making airplanes. We have all sorts of interests and ideas. Someone could just scribble on it, or simply wad it up and throw it away. Had you thought of that? *(Let the children offer ideas in as wide a variety as possible. It will help to make the point.)*

Well, we have talked about all the things that could be done, and each of those things means that you have to make a choice. If I choose to write a story on my paper, I can't cut it up and make paper snow. I have to choose what I want to do.

Each person at the meeting had to say, "At the end of this half hour, what will I have done with my paper?"—just as we made decisions about what we would do with it.

Here is the point I would like to make: Each morning God gives us a brand new day, just like this clean sheet of paper. Then we choose what we will do with the day, as it goes by. Patti disagrees. She says she had to go to school and that's not her choice. That is true. But you can make lots of choices after you get to school. You can decide if you are going to learn something or ignore the teacher. You can chose to read a good book or throw it through the window. *(The children may make several suggestions as to options, once they see the choices.)*

I think you get the idea. I would like to suggest that before you do anything, you stop and say to yourself that this job, or this day is a clean sheet of paper. What do I want on it when it is finished? Do I want it scribbled up and all full of mistakes, or do I want it well written and something I'll feel good about? If you make that decision before you begin, it will help direct you through all your activities, and you will probably feel much better when you are finished.

Turn Off the Lights

TEXT: The purpose in a man's mind is like deep water, but a man of understanding will draw it out. *Proverbs 20:5*

OBJECT: A light bulb screwed into a socket, which has an obvious switch that can be used to turn it on and off.

THRUST: We are all God's children and we need to see more than just their surface colors and sizes when we look at people.

Several years ago I went to a party with a friend, and I really had an interesting experience. There was a storm, and just as we arrived and went into the house, all the electricity went off. Have any of you ever been in a storm and had that happen? Some of you have, so you know what a strange feeling that was.

Well, there I was, in a house full of people I did not know and never had seen, and it was totally dark. I couldn't see anything. In that situation there isn't much you can do but sit down and talk to people and wait for the lights to come on. That was the part that was so interesting. When you can see people, you tend to form all sorts of ideas about what they are like, before they ever say anything. But when you cannot see them it is different. You don't know what size they are; you can't tell their age or what color they might be. You can't always be sure of their nationality, and you surely can't learn anything from the way they are dressed. All those things that so often get in the way and lead us to jump to conclusions are missing. By the time the lights came back on, I had met a lot of people, and would you believe that very few of them looked anything like I thought they would?

Have you ever thought that maybe God could solve a lot of our problems if he had a big switch like this and just turned the lights off once in a while? Then we would have to get to know people by what comes through from the inside, rather than by the superficial things we see on the outside.

This week I think it would be a great experience for you to practice listening to what is inside the people you meet. Hear what they are saying, rather than just seeing what they look like. Sense what they are feeling and get to know the persons deep inside. That was what Jesus did, and he found beautiful people everywhere.

Let's put his approach into practice and see how much we can learn from just turning off our lights that see only the outside of people, and turning on our ears and our hearts that will help us know them inside.

When God Gets Sad

TEXT: Blessed are the peacemakers, for they shall be
         called sons of God. *Matthew 5:9*

OBJECT: Two envelopes addressed to the speaker.

THRUST: The conflict between God's children is a source of
         sorrow for his Spirit.

I am sorry that things didn't work out this morning as I had
hoped. In fact, I really feel rather bad about it. I had planned to
introduce you to two friends of mine. One of them is a fine
magician, and the other tells some of the funniest stories I ever
heard. They are both fantastic people. I invited both of them,
but something unfortunate has happened. They got into a
very bad argument and each of them is very angry with the
other. In fact, they won't even speak or be in the same room
with each other. That's why they aren't here today. My real
problem is that I feel bad about it. I like both of them and I
really hate to see two people I like so much being angry with
each other.

Have any of you ever had a situation like that, when two of
your best friends became angry and didn't like each other
anymore? *(This is, of course, a very common situation, so
most of the children should be able to identify with it and
relate some type of similar experience. Take some time and let
the discussion flow. The main point is to get to the feeling
level.)* It sounds as though most of you have had a similar

experience at one time or another, and it really is sad to have your friends angry with each other, isn't it?

Have you ever thought that God might feel the same way? You know that we are all God's children, and God loves us all very much. Do you think it makes God sad when we argue or fight with one another?

(Give the children time to work with this. It may be a completely new thought and discussion may be necessary for them to work out their feelings.)

We seem to agree on at least two things. A lot of us really never thought about God being sad, but now that we have mentioned it, it does seem likely. I really think that may be the case. When there is anger or hurt feelings, everyone loses, and no one comes away feeling good. That's why God asks us to be forgiving and to be peacemakers. Sometimes it's difficult, but it is always worth it. Give that some thought this week, and see if you can be a peacemaker and help others solve problems, rather than being part of a problem yourself.

Running Through
the Woods

TEXT: I am the light of the world; he who follows me will not walk in darkness, but will have the light of life. *John 8:12*

OBJECT: A picture of a dense wooded area and a flashlight.

THRUST: God may not remove problems, but he gives us the ability to deal with them.

This morning I would like you to use your imaginations with me. I have a picture of a very dense and tangled woods. *(Let all the children get a good look at the picture so that their imaginations can work more easily.)*

I would like you to get pictures in your minds of what it would be like to walk through these woods. The trees are all around you, with roots sticking up to trip you and limbs hanging low to bump you on the head. There are bushes and vines pushing in on the trail, and they snag your coat and pull at your sleeves. Can you imagine how difficult it would be to get down a trail in those woods? *(Some of the children may want to relate some camping experiences, or they may be identifying by way of a television program. Let them share their views of the difficult nature of such a trip.)*

Well, we all seem to be in agreement that it would be hard, but I haven't told you the hardest part yet. I would like you to imagine being in those woods . . . alone . . . at night. You don't have any light, and you are running down the trail. Can you imagine that—running through these branches and bushes and things at night, with no light? What do you think that would be like?

(*Let the children truly get into it and imagine the real emotional aspect.*) John says it would be scary. Craig says you would get all banged up. Why is that? Because of running into trees and bushes, and tripping over roots and rocks? That really would be rough. Can you imagine running into a thorn bush at full speed because it is too dark to see it? That really would be bad.

Now, if we were wise campers and were given the task of running through these woods at night, what do you think we ought to take? Right! Sam hit it right off. We would take a flashlight. Why, Sam? (*Let the child or children discuss the difference the light would make.*)

You have made a good case for having a flashlight. I would like you to notice something very interesting. When you get out your flashlight and light up the trail, all the bushes and low limbs and things don't just vanish. They still are there, and you still could run into them. Then what is the difference? Right! Now you have light and can avoid them. That really does make a great difference.

In fact, that is exactly what I would like you to think about this morning. Sometimes we are asked that very question about Jesus. What difference does he make? How can he help? I think he helps a lot just as that flashlight does in the forest. Sometimes it seems that life is like running in the dark, with problems hitting us from every side. I think it is true that in some cases God simply may remove the problem, but I think that in most cases he gives us a light. He shows us how to deal with things in a way that makes us able to handle them. He shows us how to avoid getting into places and situations that will hurt us. Jesus said, "I am the light of the world." Let's follow the light he gives us and see how much smoother our paths will be.

Let's Make a Person!

TEXT: Then the Lord God formed man of dust from the ground . . . and breathed into his nostrils the breath of life; and man became a living being. *Genesis 2:7*

OBJECT: Clay.

THRUST: God is the giver of life.

I have something with me this morning that I am sure all of you will recognize. Right! It's clay, and we can use it to make all sorts of things. I am sure many of you have used clay. What kinds of things have you made? (*Let the children describe a wide variety of creations. The more they get into it, the easier it will be to make your point later.*)

It sounds as if most of you have made things from clay at one time or another. What would you suggest we make this morning? (*Get as many suggestions as possible; then go with the majority suggestion of something living.*)

Some of you want horses or cows, but it sounds as if most of you would like a person. I am going to see what kind of person we can get out of this clay. (*Remember the object is not to demonstrate your expertise as a sculptor. Use this creating process as a time to have some fun with the children.*)

There he is. Now we have a person. Is there anything else we can do? John says we can put a hat on him. Nikki wants him to have a briefcase. (*Again, accept as many suggestions as possible.*)

All right, there is our man. Now, there is one more thing we need to do to really make him just right. Who can tell me what it is? *(Accept as many suggestions as they will offer in the first rush of answers, but don't draw it into a guessing game. That only leads to frustration.)*

Well, you have made a lot of really good suggestions but no one has mentioned the thing I had in mind. We need to make him alive. If we do that, we can talk with him and really have a good time. *(Give the children time for a full response.)*

Most of you seem to feel that is impossible. We can't make him come alive. Is that what you are saying? We can give him a shape, clothes, and everything else, but we can't give him life. Well, you are right. Life, not only for people, but for all things, is a very special gift from God. He is the one who gives it, and once it is lost, we can't give it back.

That may give us something to think about when we are around things that are alive—not only people, but plants and animals, as well. Life in any form is a very special thing, and we should be very careful about how we treat living things. That is especially true with people. Each person is a special creation of God, and God loves that person just as he loves you. So let's practice being aware of the way we treat living things and of ways to protect the gift of life that God has given, especially in other persons.

This week, see what you can do to help living things live better and what you can do to make another person's life happier.

Removing Obstructions

TEXT: Wash yourselves; make yourselves clean; remove the evil of your doings from before my eyes; cease to do evil. *Isaiah 1:16*

OBJECT: A drinking straw with some type of obstruction in it (a tiny piece of "play dough" would do nicely), and a pipe cleaner longer than the straw.

THRUST: Sometimes things can block our conversations with God—but we can remove those blocks.

This morning I have something I know all of you are familiar with and probably have used. As you can see, it is a straw. Has everyone used one or know what it is for? *(This question is primarily directed at the younger ones, in an effort to be sure they are included in all aspects of the conversation. Several of the children may want to share some experiences with straws. If so, let them talk—what they say may be used to illustrate the point later.)*

Well, it seems that nearly all of you have used a straw, and everyone knows how. Todd says it is his favorite way to drink chocolate milk.

Can I ask one of you to help me with this straw for just a second? *(The children usually are quick to volunteer, so be sure, over the weeks, to include all of them in one way or another.)*

Leslie, if you will help, I would like to try an experiment. Will you take the straw and show us how it works? *(Let your helper try to suck some air through the straw. It will take only a second to discover the blockage and relate the problem.)*

What's the matter? You stopped. *(By this time, the child not only will tell you the problem, but probably will be telling the others as well.)*

You say you can't get any air through the straw? That can't be right. I thought we all agreed that a straw is made for the exact purpose of drawing things like air and liquid through it. If that's what it's made for, why isn't it working? *(Let the children explain the problem. Some of them may want to look in the straw and see where it is blocked. Someone may take the obstruction out; if so, that is fine. If no one does, you might take the following approach.)*

That thing blocking the straw really messes it up. What can we do about it? *(There may be a variety of suggestions. Let them list as many as possible.)* Jeff says to throw it away. That's one thing we could do. Wendy says we can break it. Kelli says we can run this pipe cleaner through it, remove the blockage, and still have a good straw. Would you like to try that? O.K. Amanda, will you do that for us? *(Let the child clear the straw and demonstrate how well it works.)* Great! Amanda did a good job. In fact, you all did a fine bit of thinking on that one. Now our straw is as good as new and can do all the things it was made for.

Now, there is something I think we can learn from this problem that is very important. It has to do with prayer. For just a moment I would like you to think of prayer as a kind of straw. It is designed to get something from us to God, and from God to us. To do that, there has to be an open, free-flowing passage, such as this straw. But sometimes, something happens to block the passage. We begin to pray, but something isn't right. The prayer just does not seem to get through. Have you ever had that feeling? *(Some of the children may want to comment at this point. Their illustrations can be helpful.)*

103

I have discovered that when my prayers are like that, there usually is a certain thing that is blocking my willingness or ability to hear God, just as something blocked the straw. Sometimes it's something I have done, or it may be something I didn't do, but should have. Either way, it is a block between me and God, and just as with the straw, if I want things to work right, I have to change something. God is always there to help, but I have to be willing to remove the blocks. Once I do, everything works fine again.

So I would like you to remember the lesson of the straw and keep the line open between you and God. If it does close, look for the block and remove it. Then love and friendship can always flow freely between you and God.

I'm on the Team!

TEXT: And I heard the voice of the Lord saying, "Whom shall I send, and who will go for us?" Then I said, "Here am I! Send me." *Isaiah 6:8*

OBJECT: Baseball hat, glove, and shirt.

THRUST: There is a difference between being on the team and actually playing the game.

(One of the exciting experiences for children is being on a team or in some type of group. They love uniforms and the feeling of belonging.)

I have some things with me this morning that you may recognize. *(Hold up the items where everyone can see them.)* Does everyone know what these are? Doug and David do. They are part of a baseball uniform. Right? We have the shirt, the hat, and the glove. Do any of you play on a team of any kind? *(Some of your older children may be having their first organized-team experience, but all of them have been on teams in the neighborhood or at school. It should be no problem for the children to identify with the idea.)*

I would like to tell you about a frustrating experience I had one time when I was about the age some of you are. I tried out for a baseball team and I made it. I was really happy! I went to practice and did everything the coach said. We practiced for three weeks, and then came the big day! We were going to our first game, and I was ready. You know how it feels before that first game—nervous and everything. *(Let the children share the feeling to get them really in the mood.)*

Well, I got there, I was ready, and I had quite a day . . . sitting on the bench. I not only didn't get to play, I didn't even get to stand up! You can imagine how I felt! Really bad. Did any of you ever have that happen? *(Some of the children may have had similar experiences, and their telling of them may help the others identify. It also may be a good experience for the children to have a safe place to express their disappointment.)*

Well, I'll tell you what—that was the last time I spent the whole game sitting on the bench. The next game, you know what I did? I stood up twice just for exercise. That's right! I spent the next game on the bench, too. In fact, I spent most of the season there, and I was miserable the whole time. Have any of you ever had the feeling that you never will get in a game? You seem to spend your whole life sitting and watching. *(Let the children share their feelings again.)*

Well, it sounds as though none of you like sitting on the bench any more than I did. So I wonder if you could imagine that someone is on a team and is asked to play one of the most important positions, and then just sits there on the bench and says, "I don't want to play." Can you imagine that? *(The children should respond to that without any coaching at all. Let their comments go on, since they will reinforce the point later.)*

We all agree that we can't understand why anyone would not want to do their part, especially if it is such a vital one. But I am wondering if we might be talking about one of you? *(Pause for effect.)* Some of you look surprised.

Let me put it this way. Each of us has been asked to be a part of a team. It's called God's kingdom, and its purpose is to change the world and the lives of everyone in it; to continue today all the things that Jesus began; to help people find God;

and to share with them the love that God offers. It's a great team and a wonderful and important job. But the question is this: Are we active on the team, or are we just sitting on the bench? Which are you doing in the game? It really is an important question, because if we just sit on the bench, all those people who are so much in need of what we can share, won't have it. That would be a real shame.

This week, be aware of all the chances you have to help other people, and make sure you don't put yourself on the bench. Jump into God's game and see how great it is to share that love with others.

Possibilities Unlimited

TEXT: As for what was sown on good soil, this is he who hears the word and understands it; he indeed bears fruit, and yields, in one case a hundredfold, in another sixty, and in another thirty.
Matthew 13:23

OBJECT: An apple that has been cut in half.

THRUST: In one apple we have the potential for unlimited apples. The same is true of our talents.

I know that all of you are good in math, so you will have no problem with my question this morning. *(Hold the apple in such a way that it appears to be uncut.)* How many apples do I have in my hand? Everyone seems to agree—there is only one. Basically, I guess you are right. But watch very carefully. *(Let the apple come apart; then lift two or three seeds to the surface.)*

Who will tell me what those are? Sarah, that's right. They are seeds. Now, here is my next question. We can see how many seeds are in this apple, but who can tell me how many apples are in these seeds? *(At first the question may make no sense to the younger ones, so you will need to expand.)*

What I mean is this. I have one apple, but this apple has eight seeds. Now if I plant these eight seeds and get eight apple trees, each tree will grow hundreds of new apples—right? In each of those hundreds of apples, there will be more seeds that can make more trees. If the process goes on and on, how many apples can be produced from just this one that I have in my hand? *(The children have had only limited experience with large numbers, but you will get some good answers.)*

Linda, I hear you saying that it is impossible to tell. It could keep going on forever. There is no limit to how many trees and apples could come from just this one. Somehow this little apple begins to look a lot more important to me—how about you? *(Let the children respond so you can be sure they have grasped the idea.)*

The idea I want to share with you this morning is that if this is true of apples, it is true of other things, also. For example, we may have a chance to do something nice for someone and share God's love. But then we might say, it's only a small thing, like the apple, so what difference could it make? Yet, if we do it, we may discover that our kind act really is like the apple. It has in it the seeds to produce an unlimited amount of kindness that can spread and grow. When we are kind to someone, they feel better, so they treat others better. Then they in turn pass it on, and it all started when you planted the seed. This week, see how many trees of kindness you can start, and then enjoy watching them grow.

The
Most Important Day
of the Year

TEXT: This is the day which the Lord has made; let us rejoice and be glad in it.   *Psalm 118:24*

OBJECT: A calendar with several special days marked.

THRUST: Today is the most important day of your life, because it is the only day you can control.

One of the things we really enjoy around our house is a calendar. We have many different kinds, with pictures and sayings and little reminders written all through them. How many of you have calendars around your house? Oh, good! Lots of you do. They really are nice, aren't they? (*Let some of the children share their thoughts about the calendars they have or enjoy.*)

You know that calendars have lots of purposes, but the main one is to tell us what day it is. As you can see on the one I have, here, there are all sorts of special days marked in red and others, in blue. It is amazing how many special days there are on some calendars. We have one at home that has two or three special names and celebrations indicated on each day of the whole year. Can you think of some special days during the year? (*Let the children begin compiling a list.*)

We are getting quite a list here. Let's do it this way. What do you think is the most important day of the year? (*You will get all sorts of suggestions and reasons for them. Let the children have some fun with it.*)

110

We have lots of different opinions, so I will tell you the day I think is most important. It's today, whatever the date might be. The thing I have discovered is that yesterday is gone, and there is nothing I can do about that. It never can be changed, no matter what. On the other hand, tomorrow is still coming, and I can't actually do anything with it until it gets here. That leaves me with today. It's the only day I have when I can shape or use the time for any purpose. If today is *all* I have, then it becomes the most *important* day, doesn't it? *(The children usually will not have any difficulty grasping the concept and probably can offer several illustrations.)*

I think you all understand what I am thinking, and I would like you to remember it as you go through this week. Begin to use each day to its fullest and enjoy all the good things God has given you. And take full advantage of the opportunities you have to share his love with others.

What If
You Could Feed
Ten Thousand People?

TEXT: When it was evening, the disciples came to him and said, "This is a lonely place, and the day is now over; send the crowds away to go into the villages and buy food for themselves." Jesus said, "They need not go away; you give them something to eat." They said to him, "We have only five loaves here and two fish." And he said, "Bring them here to me." Then he ordered the crowds to sit down on the grass; and taking the five loaves and the two fish he looked up to heaven, and blessed, and broke and gave the loaves to the disciples, and the disciples gave them to the crowds. And they all ate and were satisfied. And they took up twelve baskets full of the broken pieces left over. And those who ate were about five thousand men, besides women and children. *Matthew 14:15-21*

OBJECT: A package of seeds and some pictures of hungry people.

THRUST: We can take the money we spend for one movie and use it to buy seeds that can grow food for 10,000 people.

Have you ever heard the part of the Bible in which Jesus told his followers that they would do even greater things than he did (John 14:12)? When we think of some of the things he did, that really would be something, wouldn't it? *(Let the children ponder the thought for a moment. It may take a second to register.)*

This morning I am thinking about one particular thing that Jesus did. It seems that a lot of people had followed him out into the country to listen to what he was saying. When he finished, they suddenly realized that they had missed lunch, and everyone was really hungry. The Bible tells us that Jesus was concerned about the people, and so he took some loaves and fish and fed them. It was really amazing then, but it seems even more fantastic when we think that he told us to do the same sort of thing. Can you imagine having five thousand in for lunch? If one of us ate three times a day it would take almost five years to eat that many meals. This is a tremendous amount of food, yet Jesus said that we can do even greater things. How could we feed that many people? *(Let the children offer whatever suggestions they may have. You might be surprised at the validity of the solutions and ideas.)*

I have heard a number of good ideas, and I believe several of them might work. Here's another idea that will work, if we all help. *(Show them the package of seeds. We used corn because of the number of things that can be made from it and because several of the children had planted the seeds.)* How many of you have fifty cents in your banks at home? Lots of you do! Well, there are about thirty of us here, so if we joined together and each gave just fifty cents, we could buy sixteen dollars' worth of corn seed. If we sent that as part of our outreach offering, and it was planted, each seed would produce a stalk of corn with four or five ears, and each ear would have dozens of seeds on it. There would be enough to help feed an entire village, and still some left to plant for another crop next year. We would be using a different method, but we would be doing exactly what Jesus talked about. Just the seeds from our little group would be helping to feed thousands of people, many of whom have no food at all. That makes it very important, doesn't it?

This next week, while we are getting ready for our special outreach offering, think about the children who have nothing to eat, and remember that Jesus tells us to feed them. He loves them, just as he loves us, and he wants us to share with them. Let's see how many seeds we can buy, and how many people we can invite to lunch when we really want to.

It's Your Move!

TEXT: I can do all things in him who strengthens me. *Philippians 4:13*

OBJECT: A chess set.

THRUST: We are free in Christ to become anything we want to be.

This morning I have something with me that some of you may not recognize. It is a chess set. How many of you have seen the pieces before and know what they are? *(Let the children respond. Some of them may want to relate some experiences, and their explanations and enthusiasm will be helpful for those children who are not familiar with chess.)*

Well, from the comments, I guess some of you even have begun playing chess a little. *(Let them relate experiences again.)* Julie says she is learning, but it is hard to remember how all the different pieces move. Does anyone else have that problem? *(Probably all who have tried the game will respond at this point, and that is exactly what you want.)*

I'm glad you mentioned that, because I want to talk a little bit about how some of the pieces move.

This piece is called a pawn. He can only move forward, and he has to stop if someone gets in his way. *(Don't try to go into all the variations of moves. You will lose the children immediately. By touching briefly on several pieces you will hold their interest and make your point.)*

This piece is a castle. It can move any number of squares

115

back and forth in a straight line. (*Slide the pieces to demonstrate what you are describing as you talk.*)

This piece is called the queen. She is the most powerful piece on the board. She can move any number of squares in a straight line. (*Don't use too many pieces. I usually avoid the knight because it is too difficult for the children to grasp, and it really isn't relevant to the thrust of the talk anyway.*)

As you can see, there are a lot of pieces and each can move in a different way. Each piece has a certain way it can move, and that is all it can do.

If you could be one of these pieces, which one would you like to be? (*Let the children make their selections and state why they like those particular pieces. Keep bringing the conversation back to the way the pieces move and the restrictions placed on them. Usually, after a few moments, several of the children will begin to opt more for the queen because of its obvious mobility. That is when you make the point.*)

We have several different selections, but I noticed that a lot of you chose the queen. Why was that? I see. The queen has more choice of movement and can go more places. Is that what you're telling me? Being able to move around like that gives one more freedom—right? I thought that's what you were saying. But you know, even the piece with the most freedom of movement can move only in certain ways. It is what it is, and that's that. (*I would not get into changing a pawn   .to another piece. Though even then, whatever the pawn converts to still is governed by the rules of movement.*)

Now having seen that, I would like you to think about something. When God made you, he didn't say that you can *only* be this or *only* do that. Have you ever thought about that? If we were pieces on a board, we could move anywhere. That would make us the strongest pieces in the whole game, wouldn't it? Sure. And that is exactly what God did. He has given us talents and abilities and said, "You can be whatever you want." We are free to be all we can be. That really is a great gift from God to us—the gift to grow, to learn, to be anything. And if we follow his guidance, he will help us become the very best we can be with what we have.

This week, think about all the freedom you have to grow and learn and be, and spend some time thanking God for such a wonderful gift.

A Job for Everyone

TEXT: Now there are varieties of gifts, but the same
           Spirit; and there are varieties of service, but the
           same Lord; and there are varieties of working, but
           it is the same God who inspires them all in every
           one. To each is given the manifestation of the
           Spirit for the common good.
           I Corinthians 12:4-7

OBJECT: A series of weights, from 50 pounds down to
           marbles.

THRUST: There is a job for every one of us, regardless of our
           size or ability.

*(The only caution that would be advisable is the obvious one
of not allowing some of the more enthusiastic children to hurt
themselves by trying to pick up too much. It is easy to control
this simply by handing out the weights one at a time.)*

This morning I have a number of objects with me, and I am
sure you know what many of them are. Can some of you
identify these for us? *(Some of the older children will recognize
the weights and do most of the explanation concerning their
purpose.)*

Derry has given us a good description of all the material
here, so now I will tell you what we are thinking about doing.
We are going to move all these to the storeroom in the back of
the church. I felt it would be helpful if one of you would carry
them out as you leave this morning. *(You may get several*

immediate volunteers.) The total weight is about one hundred fifty pounds. *(That may bring down a number of the hands and usually starts some impromptu discussion about dividing the load. Let it go for a few seconds, then use it to build on.)*

That really does sound pretty heavy, doesn't it? I guess it would take someone fairly big to carry that much all the way to the storeroom. I think some of you already have come up with a solution, however; Kristin and Nikki are looking for a way to divide the load among several of you. Do you think that will work? *(Let them continue their discussion on how it can be divided.)*

I think you have the answer. It is easier if everyone helps, isn't it? The thing I would like all of us to learn this morning is that *everyone* can help in this job. We have objects here that are all sizes and weights, and we can divide them in such a way that everyone can have a part. Sometimes we say, "Oh, I'm too small," or "I can't help; I'm too little." For some jobs that may be true. *(It is important to recognize the children's limitations. It is a fact that there are some things they cannot do yet, and to be told that "someday" they will be able to, simply emphasizes their current lack of ability. The concentration is on what they CAN do NOW. They should be encouraged to strive for fulfillment, but also to enjoy their accomplishments.)* But the thing to remember is that there are important jobs for everyone, no matter what our size or age. All people are important and should be allowed to help in everything, to whatever extent they can.

So this week, when you see something happening, look for things you can do to help, and then take part in what is going on.

How to Break
a Coat Hanger

TEXT: Therefore do not be anxious about tomorrow, for
           tomorrow will be anxious for itself. Let the day's
           own trouble be sufficient for the day.
           Matthew 6:34

OBJECT: A wire coat hanger.

THRUST: If at first something looks too difficult, we can
           learn to do it a little at a time.

I have something here that I know all of you have seen, but
this morning we are going to use it for a different purpose than
usual. Can I get two of you to volunteer to help me? Oh, great!
We have all sorts of help, and we may have time for several of
you to help.

We have Linda and Patti ready to begin. Now I want you to
break this coat hanger. Patti, you can pull on one end, and
Linda can pull on the other. *(Let them give it a try, but don't
let it go on too long, or it may get out of hand.)* Let's stop for a
second. It doesn't look as though it is going to break. I saw
Todd's hand up, and he is pretty big. Do you think you can
break it? Good. Give it a pull. *(Let him try it; but again, don't
let it get too wild.)* That was a great attempt, but that wire is
really strong. To tell you the truth, I don't think I could break
it, either, if I tried to pull it apart. But let me show you
something I have learned. *(Begin to bend the wire back and
forth so that eventually, it will snap.)*

How about that? Have any of you seen that done before?

Yes. Some of you have. The wire is too strong to pull apart in one big tug, so we just do it a little at a time. When we do that, it isn't hard at all.

I think we can learn something very important from our experience with this coat hanger. At one time or another, all of us are faced with jobs or problems that just seem to be much more than we can handle. Have you ever felt that way? (*Let them relate their experiences. As one child tells of having that feeling and why, the others will begin to recall similar situations. It is much more effective for the children to share this way than for the adult to try to suggest situations that may have produced such feelings. If for some reason you do not get any immediate response, you can always refer to those daily insurmountable tasks of cleaning one's room, picking up all the toys in the backyard, or drying the dishes after a big meal.*)

Now that you have had a chance to think about it, I see that many of you have had that feeling, and as things come up in the future, you may have it again. Whenever that happens, I would like you to remember two things. The first is that you always have God as a helper when you face any kind of problem. God is always there to guide and to help. Second, remember the coat hanger. It was too much to handle in one pull, so we just took it a little at a time.

I think if you will approach problems with those two things in mind, you will find them much easier to overcome. Try it this week and see how it works.

In Living Color!

TEXT: The Mighty One, God the Lord, speaks and summons the earth from the rising of the sun to its setting. Out of Zion, the perfection of beauty, God shines forth. *Psalm 50:1-2*

OBJECT: Some pictures of forests, sunsets, or flowers—some in black and white and a few in color.

THRUST: God has given us a beautiful world; let's take time to appreciate the gift and thank him for it.

I have some pictures with me that I would like to share with you. Some of them I took myself, and others I found in magazines. (*Hold up the black and white pictures of the forest or some other colorful scenery.*) This is a picture I took of some flowers in our backyard. We have roses of many different colors. There are white and pink and all different shades of red. They are really beautiful when they are blooming, as they are in this picture.

This picture (*hold up another black and white*) is one I took on vacation last year. You can see the mountains and lake. The scenery was beautiful. See all the shades of green in the forest and the blues in the lake and sky. It was fantastic! (*By this time several of the children are going to be wondering why you are showing them black and white pictures while you are referring to colors. Let them continue to wonder for a time. It is better if one of them asks the question that will lead to the next stage of the talk.*)

This picture is one that I really enjoy. (*Hold up a black and white picture of something that is extremely colorful. I chose a sunset.*) I took this last fall, just north of Liberal. You can see all the beautiful colors of the sunset glowing just over the golden wheat fields. It's really breathtaking, isn't it? (*This leading type of question usually will draw some response.*) What? Karla says she can't see the color. (*Pause a second and study the photograph.*) Well, I guess it does leave something to be desired in just black and white. It really would be more beautiful in color, wouldn't it? (*Let the children respond.*)

I have some other pictures here. (*Hold up several color shots of objects or scenes.*) Do they do more for you? I thought so. It's just a lot more pleasant to look at things in color, isn't it? What are some of your favorite colors? (*Let the children share favorite colors. Some of them may want to tell about sunsets or flowers. That's fine. It will all add to the point.*)

You all really seem to enjoy colors. Have you ever thanked God for color? I guess some of you never have thought about that. Well, I suspect a lot of people haven't. But it is a fact that God could have made the whole world and everything in it just in black and white. Think of all the beauty we would have missed. He could have done that and everything still would have worked fine. Why do you think God chose color? (*Let them talk it over for a bit.*)

I think we have a consensus. The world would have worked in black and white, yet God went ahead and added color. Maybe it was just for us to enjoy. Maybe it was God's way to help us learn to look for beauty and to enjoy life even more. I think that was really nice of God. It really is a beautiful present that will last forever. This week, as we enjoy all the colors around us, let's take some time to thank God for color. It's a wonderful gift from a wonderful God.

The Importance of Following Through

TEXT: Do you not know that in a race all the runners compete, but only one receives the prize? So run that you may obtain it. *I Corinthians 9:24*

OBJECT: A baseball bat.

THRUST: You may get off to a good start, but it is important to do more than just start; you must follow through and finish the task.

I would like to share something with you that I learned from playing baseball. When I first began to play, I wasn't a very good hitter. The pitcher would throw, and I would swing, but somehow the catcher always ended up with the ball. Have any of you ever had that experience? (*Let the children share their Little League experiences. It may help their frustration to be able to identify with others at this point.*)

Well, since some of you are having the same problem, I'll tell you what I did. I found someone I knew who was an excellent hitter. Then I watched him very carefully and tried to do all the things he did. He got a good firm grip on the bat. I watched how he stood in the batter's box. Sometimes he moved up and sometimes, back. I copied the way he spread his feet and the way he bent his knees. Then I started working on my swing. He had a great cut at the ball. He followed through with his whole body. I was really impressed! The season before, he had hit thirty home runs! That was way more than anyone else had hit.

Well, I watched him, and I copied what he did. I really worked at it. And do you know what happened? *(Some of the children may want to guess. Have some fun and see what they decide.)*

Some of you almost guessed it. Paul was right. I did hit the ball! In fact, I hit it so far, I couldn't believe it! I stood there and watched it go and go and go. I felt so good I turned to the catcher and said, "Did you see that?" Boy, I felt good! *(You may be getting some response from the children by this time.)* But do you know what happened? *(You should get several answers.)* Right. They threw me out at first! I had spent so much time feeling good about my great hit that I never got around to running the bases. That does seem a little silly, doesn't it? *(Most of the children will be with you on that score!)*

After that happened, I realized that something very important could be learned from it, and I'll share it with you. I think we all agree that hitting the ball is a very important thing to do in a baseball game. But while it is an important beginning, it is *only* a beginning. After we hit the ball—even if we hit it over the fence—we still have to run the bases. So what I learned is this: Starting is important, but it's finishing that really counts.

I would like you to remember that, when you begin your next project or the next time you decide to do something. Frequently, we will be talking to God and we will feel that he wants us to do something; then we get really excited. We talk about it, and do lots of planning, and jump in with all we have, and then somehow, we sort of fizzle out. At times like that, remember our talk. God continues to give us guidance and strength, so let's stay with him the whole way and get the job done.

Loved to Pieces

TEXT: A new commandment I give to you, that you love one another; even as I have loved you, that you also love one another. By this all men will know that you are my disciples. *John 13:34-35*

OBJECT: Two stuffed animals—one in good condition and the other, old and totally worn.

THRUST: Loving is giving of oneself to others.

I have two objects with me this morning that I know you will recognize. *(Show them the animals.)* How many of you have stuffed animals at home? That's neat. Do you have some favorites? *(Let the children talk freely about their favorite animals. Their affection for the animal is the thrust, so they well may make your entire point.)*

I would like to tell you something about these two animals. This one *(the one in better condition)* is a rabbit that has been at the house for about two years. It really is in great shape for being around that long. This duck has been around a little longer. *(Show them the worn-out one.)* It's been there three or four years. I'm sure you can see there is a bit of difference between them.

Now, without my saying any more, which one would you say was loved most? *(This may lead to an interesting discussion and maybe to some real insights with your children.)*

Matthew and Ricky both have come to an interesting conclusion. They said that the rabbit is in the best condition, so it probably has had less use. That means the duck actually was handled more, and so it must be the one that was most loved. I see several of you nodding your heads. Does that mean you agree? Well, you happen to be exactly right. The duck was a real favorite. It was carried everywhere. It went to play, it came to the table, it was part of going to bed, it even made it to the bathtub a few times. Have some of you had a favorite like that? (*Let them share their favorites again.*) I thought so. You have some like the duck, just loved more than anything. In fact, I would be willing to bet that if you have a favorite toy like this duck, you don't think of it as a toy at all. It is a real friend, isn't it? (*You are entering into an area of tremendous possibilities, if the children will share their feelings with you.*)

What I hear you saying is when something has been loved like our friend the duck has been, a wonderful thing happens. It becomes real, and there are special feelings that are shared; feelings we don't have for just "anyone." That really is true. The important thing is that it also is true of people.

Sometimes we think people are "real" just because they are there and we can see them. That's the difference between a mere existence and the abundant living that Jesus talked about. That also is why Jesus told us that as Christians, we are to practice the great art of sharing love and acceptance with others. That's the way we make people real. We help them step into that wonderful world of feeling good about being God's child and of sharing that feeling freely with others.

This week, get to know someone better—maybe even someone in your own family. See if by loving and being loved, both of you might experience the joy of being real.